THE WRITINGS
OF CLARE OF ASSISI

LETTERS, FORM OF LIFE,
TESTAMENT AND BLESSING

STUDIES IN EARLY FRANCISCAN SOURCES

VOLUME 3

General Editors

Michael W. Blastic, O.F.M.,
Jay M. Hammond, Ph.D.,
J.A. Wayne Hellmann, O.F.M. Conv.

The Writings of Clare of Assisi

Letters, Form of Life, Testament and Blessing

Studies in Early Franciscan Sources

Volume 3

Edited by
Michael W. Blastic, O.F.M.,
Jay M. Hammond, Ph.D.,
J.A. Wayne Hellmann, O.F.M. Conv.

FRANCISCAN
INSTITUTE
PUBLICATIONS

St. Bonaventure, New York

Published in the United States by Franciscan Institute Publications
St. Bonaventure University
St. Bonaventure, NY 14778

Cover design by Books & Projects LLC.
Cover art from the Dossal of St. Clare of Assisi
Basilica of Santa Clara, Assisi

ISBN 10: 1-57659-233-2
ISBN 13: 978-1-57659-233-5

Library of Congress Cataloging-in-Publication Data

Clare, of Assisi, Saint, 1194-1253.
  [Selections. 2011]
  The writings of Clare of Assisi : letters, form of life, testament
and blessing / edited by Michael W. Blastic, Jay M. Hammond,
and J.A. Wayne Hellmann.
        p. cm. -- (Studies in early Franciscan sources ; v. 3)
  Includes bibliographical references.
  ISBN 978-1-57659-233-5 (hardcover) -- ISBN 978-1-57659-233-5
(paperback) -- ISBN 978-1-57659-298-4 (e-book)
  1. Clare, of Assisi, Saint, 1194-1253. 2. Spiritual life--Catholic
Church--Early works to 1800. I. Title.
  BX2179.C57E5 2011
  271'.97302--dc23
                                                      2011018841

Printed in the United States of America
By BookMasters, Inc.
Ashland, Ohio

CONTENTS

INTRODUCTION

Building on the scholarly research of the last half of the twentieth century, the first decade of the twenty-first century has provided new translations of the writings of Clare into modern languages. In the English speaking world, the volume, *Clare of Assisi: Early Documents – The Lady*[1] provides new possibilities for those who are interested in reading the writings of Saint Clare. During the last ten years, translating the writings and hagiography of Clare has become an international project. This is why the series *Introduction to Early Franciscan Sources* has begun.

As of 2010 the task is to learn how to read, interpret, and apply these newly translated texts to enrich the historical understanding, theological vision, and practical living out of the Gospel message. However, the question remains: how does one get started? This third volume aims to provide assistance to those interested in deeper understanding of the writings of Clare. Hence, the volume contains essays on the known texts written by or about her. The authors, scholars interested in and committed to the Franciscan tradition, have brought contemporary research together, applied it to each of the specific texts, and offered their own perspective.

The essays make available a new resource for further study and interpretation in two ways. First, the essays define the *status questionis* by informing the reader about the state of current research on each of the texts considered. Hopefully, this will help the reader find a point of departure for either interpreting the texts or for moving the research forward. Second, the essays are intended to introduce the reader to these texts within the dimensions of their multilayered contextual-historical framework. Hopefully, this will open the door for solid theological

---

[1] *Clare of Assisi: Early Documents, The Lady*, Regis Armstrong, ed. and trans. (New York: New City Press, 2006).

reflection, the only foundation for further development of Franciscan spirituality.

What Does This Volume Contain?

The volume contains the writings of Clare. Her writings are not presented historically or chronologically. Rather, the essays are ordered thematically according to the genre of the writings. However, each essay contextualizes the considered text within its own historical framework. Accordingly, the historical context is foundational to each essay.

The presentation of historical context within each essay generally considers four perspectives. Consideration of these four perspectives is crucial for understanding and interpreting historical texts. These perspectives are the following:

1. There is the historical context of time and place that actually situates the text in its origins. For example, when and why was the text written? What were its social underpinnings?

2. There is the question of the transmission of the text or how did it develop from its origin to our own day. The study of the manuscript tradition considers the text as an historical artifact. This is called the codicological context. For example, how did the text survive, how did its migration through the centuries change the text, and how do we know it is authentic?

3. The receptive context identifies how scholars of more recent times have accepted and interpreted the text. For example, how do modern scholars read the text, and what questions do they ask of the text?

4. Finally, there is the context of Clare herself. This involves a study of how these text provide insight into the life of Clare and her community, and, at the same time, how these texts give crystallized expression of the Clarian life itself. For example, how is authorship understood? Along with the related questions of intertextuality, e.g., how does an earlier *Letter of Clare to Agnes* condition the interpretation of a later letter?

Awareness of these inter-related and multivalent contexts are foundational for an informed reading of these medieval texts. Because of this, the authors developed their essays with these perspectives in mind, as will be apparent.

How Are the Essays Structured?

Each essay examines a text or group of texts with the same general fourfold pattern: *Establishing the Text, Approaching the Text, Interpreting the Text*, and *Bibliography*. While this fourfold pattern provides uniformity among the various essays, the specific execution of the essays varies according to the nature of and scholarship about particular texts. In other words, the fourfold pattern intentionally provides uniform categories while allowing for flexibility in the summaries and analysis.

- *Establishing the Text* examines the current status of the manuscript tradition and modern critical editions upon which modern translations are based. Likewise, this section, if pertinent, addresses issues regarding authorship and explanation of the genres of the texts under consideration.

- *Approaching the Text* generally presents the text's historical context, and the sources utilized within the text. Again, if pertinent, this section also surveys modern studies of the text and identifies unresolved questions surrounding the study of the text.

- *Interpreting the Text*, outlines the text's structure that organizes the material and also identifies significant themes, symbols, and images that encode the text's meaning within its structure. Often this third section ends with a consideration of the text's significance.

- The *Bibliography*, provides reference to the manuscript tradition, critical editions, modern translations, at least in English, and key secondary studies that explore various issues in the text under consideration.

With these four categories, the volume attempts to examine the various interrelated contexts that surround the investigation of the text that emerge out of a specific thirteenth-century social/religious movement that underwent rapid and dramatic development.

What is the Wider Context?

Although the essays in this volume strive to provide the background for understanding the various contexts for specific texts, as well as bibliographies for those texts, the essays presuppose a familiarity with the story of Clare, as well as with the history of the early Franciscan movement. The following resources can help the reader become familiar with the more general medieval Franciscan context.

The Franciscan Movement

Carmody, Maurice. *The Franciscan Story: St. Francis of Assisi and His Influence since the Thirteenth Century*. London: Athena Press, 2008.

Flood, David. *Francis of Assisi and the Franciscan Movement*. Quezon City: FIA Contact Publications, 1989.

Iriarte, Lazio. *Franciscan History: The Three Orders of St. Francis of Assisi*. Trans. Patricia Ross, with an appendix, "The Historical Context of the Franciscan Movement," by Lawrence C. Landini. Chicago: Franciscan Herald Press, 1982.

Merlo, Grado Giovanni. *In the Name of St. Francis: History of the Friars Minor and Franciscanism until the Early Sixteenth Century*. Trans. Raphael Bonnano. Ed. Robert J. Karris and Jean François Godet-Calogeras. St. Bonaventure, NY: Franciscan Institute Publications, 2009.

Moorman, John. *A History of the Franciscan Order from its Origins to the Year 1517*. Oxford: Oxford University Press, 1968. Chicago: Franciscan Herald Press, 1988; reprint of 1965 edition; St. Bonaventure, NY: Franciscan Institute Publications, 2007.

Robson, Michael. *The Franciscans in the Middle Ages*. Woodbridge: The Boydell Press, 2006.

Clare of Assisi

Alberzoni, Maria Pia. *Clare of Assisi and the Poor Sisters in the Thirteenth Century*. St. Bonaventure, NY: Franciscan Institute Publications, 2004.

Bartoli, Marco. *Clare of Assisi*. Trans. Frances Teresa. Quincy, IL: Franciscan Press, 1993.

Mueller, Joan. *The Privilege of Poverty: Clare of Assisi, Agnes of Prague, and the Struggle for a Franciscan Rule for Women*. University Park, PA: Pennsylvania State University, 2006.

DEDICATION

To the Franciscans who have made this volume possible
through their modern critical editions
of Francis and Clare:

Leonhard Lemmens

Kajetan Esser

Giovanni Boccali

Carlo Paolazzi

Marie-France Becker

Jean-François Godet-Calogeras

Thaddée Matura

ACKNOWLEDGEMENTS

The editors wish to express their gratitude for the assistance of
Saint Louis University graduate students Benjamin O'Conner,
Robert Rexroat, and Catherine Scine of the Department
of Theological Studies. Peter Nickels, O.F.M. Conv., proofread
all the essays. Daria Mitchell of the Franciscan Institute at Saint
Bonaventure University was most helpful in the preparation of the
manuscript.

ABBREVIATIONS

WRITINGS OF SAINT FRANCIS

1Frg   Fragments of Worchester Manuscript
1LtCl   First Letter to the Clergy (Earlier Edition)
1LtCus   The First Letter to the Custodians
1LtF   The First Letter to the Faithful
2Frg   Fragments of Thomas of Celano
2LtCl   Second Letter to the Clergy (Later Edition)
2LtCus   The Second Letter to the Custodians
2LtF   The Second Letter to the Faithful
3Frg   Fragments from Hugh of Digne
Adm   The Admonitions
BlL   A Blessing for Brother Leo
CtC   The Canticle of the Creatures
CtExh   The Canticle of Exhortation
ER   The Earlier Rule (*Regula non bullata*)
ExhP   Exhortation to the Praise of God
LR   The Later Rule (*Regula bullata*)
LtAnt   A Letter to Brother Anthony of Padua
LtL   A Letter to Brother Leo
LtMin   A Letter to a Minister
LtOrd   A Letter to the Entire Order
LtR   A Letter to Rulers of the Peoples
OfP   The Office of the Passion
PrCr   The Prayer before the Crucifix
PrOF   A Prayer Inspired by the Our Father
PrsG   The Praises of God
PrsH   Praises for All the Hours
RH   A Rule for Hermitages

SalBV   A Salutation of the Blessed Virgin Mary
SalV   A Salutation of Virtues
Test   The Testament
TPJ   True and Perfect Joy

WRITINGS OF CLARE OF ASSISI

1LAg   The First Letter to Agnes of Prague
2LAg   The Second Letter to Agnes of Prague
3LAg   The Third Letter to Agnes of Prague
4LAg   The Fourth Letter to Agnes of Prague
LEr   The Letter to Ermentrudge of Brudges
FLCl   The Form of Life
BlCl   The Blessing

FRANCISCAN SOURCES

1-3JT   The Praises by Jacopone da Todi
1-4Srm The Sermons of Bonaventure
1C   The Life of Saint Francis by Thomas of Celano
1MP   The Mirror of Perfection, Smaller Version
2C   The Remembrance of the Desire of a Soul
2MP   The Mirror of Perfection, Larger Version
3C   The Treatise on the Miracles by Thomas of Celano
AC   The Assisi Compilation
AP   The Anonymous of Perugia
BCCl   The Bull of Canonization for Saint Clare
BCFr   The Bull of Canonization for Saint Francis
BPr   The Book of Praises by Bernard of Besse
ChrJG   The Chronicle of Jordan of Giano
ChrTE   The Chronicle of Thomas of Eccleston
DBF   The Deeds of Blessed Francis and His Companions
DCom   The Divine Comedy by Dante Alighieri
FLHug   The Form of Life provided by Cardinal Hugolino
FLInn   The Form of Life provided by Pope Innocent IV

CONTRIBUTORS

MICHAEL W. BLASTIC, O.F.M., is a Friar Minor of the Holy Name of Jesus Province, New York, NY. He is presently an Associate Professor and the Chair of Franciscan Theology and Spirituality Studies at the Washington Theological Union, Washington DC. He received his Ph.D. in Historical Theology from St. Louis University, St. Louis, Missouri. His research and publications focus on the Writings of Francis and Clare of Assisi, the Franciscan Hagiographical Tradition, and the early Franciscan tradition of theology and spirituality.

JEAN FRANÇOIS GODET-CALOGERAS, PH. D. is a Franciscan scholar internationally known for his publications on the early Franciscan documents, in particular the writings of Francis and Clare of Assisi. A native of Belgium, Jean François received his education in classical philology and medieval studies at the Catholic University of Louvain. In the early 1980s he facilitated the international work group which elaborated the text of the new Rule of the Third Order Regular. Jean François has resided in the USA since 1991, and currently serves as full professor at the Franciscan Institute/School of Franciscan Studies, Saint Bonaventure University.

LEZLIE KNOX, PH. D. (1999) in Medieval Studies, University of Notre Dame, is Assistant Professor of History at Marquette University. She has published extensively on Clare of Assisi and the Franciscan sisters during the Middle Ages. In 2002-03, she received an ACL/Mellon Fellowship for Junior Faculty. She contributed "What Francis Intended: Gender and the Transmission of Knowledge in the Fransciscan Order" to *Seeing and Knowing: Women and Learning in Medieval Europe, 1200-1500*, ed. Anneke Mulder-Bakker (Brepols, 2004). In 2008, Brill published her monograph entitled *Creating Clare of Assisi: Female Franciscan Identities in Later Medieval Italy*.

INGRID PETERSON, O.S.F. is a Franciscan sister from Rochester, Minnesota. She has an undergraduate degree from The College of Saint Teresa, an M.A. in public address from the University of Michigan in Ann Arbor, and a Ph. D. in English with a concentration in medieval literature from the University of Iowa. She taught graduate level courses on medieval women, Clare of Assisi, and the Franciscan mystical tradition at the Franciscan Institute, Saint Bonaventure University and the Franciscan International Study Centre in Canterbury, England. She has written *Clare of Assisi: a Biographical Study* published by Franciscan Press, Quincy, Illinois and co-authored *Praying with Clare of Assisi* with Ramona Miller. In 2001, Ingrid was given the Franciscan Institute Medal for outstanding scholarship in Franciscan studies, to date the only woman to be so honored.

Clare of Assisi's Letters to Agnes of Prague: Testaments of Fidelity

Ingrid Peterson

I. Establishing the Text

Manuscripts

In 1982 the name of Clare of Assisi (1193-1253) emerged onto the front pages of Franciscan scholarship in the English-speaking world with the publication of *Francis and Clare: The Complete Works*, edited and translated by Regis J. Armstrong and Ignatius Brady in the Paulist Press Classics of Western Spirituality series.[1] I. Omaechevarria's 1970 *Escritos de Santa Clara y Documentos Complentarios* collected together and published the Latin texts, as well as a Spanish translation of Clare's four *Letters to Agnes of Prague*, a *Letter to Ermentrude of Bruges*, the *Form of Life*, *Testament*, and *Blessing*.[2] In 1976 Giovanni Boccali prepared a critical edition of the Latin texts which included the writings of both Francis and Clare, *Textus opusculorum S. Francisci et S. Clarae Assisiensium*.[3] In 1953 at the time of the seventh centenary of Clare's death, Damien Vorreux's French translation of Clare's writings

---

[1] *Francis and Clare: The Complete Works*, ed. and trans. Regis J. Armstrong and Ignatius Brady (New York: Paulist Press, 1982).

[2] I. Omaechevarria, *Escritos de Santa Clara y documentos contemporáneos* (Madrid, 1970).

[3] Giovanni Boccali, *Textus opusculorum S. Francisci et S. Clarae Assisiensium* (Assisi: S. Maria de Angeli, 1976).

were published as *Sainte Claire d'Assise; Sa Vie par Thomas de Celano; Ses Écrits.*[4]

In 1985, Marie-France Becker, Jean François Godet, and Thaddée Matura edited *Claire d'Assise: Écrits* which interfaced the Latin texts with the French translations as well as providing an extensive introduction, a full complement of scholarly apparatus, and an index to assist in studying Clare's writings.[5] This volume followed the format of the series, Sources Chrétiennes, a collection of Greek and Latin Christian texts from the patristic and medieval periods. Volume 325 contains Clare's *Four Letters to Agnes of Prague,* "Form of Life," "Testament" and "Blessing." Soon other language groups produced similar editions of translations of Clare's writings and essential related texts complete with a variety of appended material.

To date, no critical edition of the Latin texts of the body of Clare's writings has been produced. While the source texts for *Claire d'Assise: Écrits* are not from critical editions, the original Latin texts were critically established in that they were based on the most recent manuscript research. The writings of Francis translated from Kajetan Esser's text had previously been published in 1981 in this same series as volume 285.[6] Today Clare of Assisi continues to remain in the foreground of the Franciscan world stage.

Editions and Translations

Until the beginning of the twentieth century, only the Bohemian version of the letters by J. Plachy, printed in 1566 and the Latin text published in 1668 of the *Acta Sanctorum* were known.[7] In addition, in 1491 Nicholas Glassberger made a copy of the Latin text of the First Letter which appears in the manuscript, *Cronica XXIV Generalium Or-*

---

[4] *Écrits* 15, n. 15, cites Damien Vorreux, in *Sainte Claire d'Assise; Sa Vie par Thomas de Celano; Ses Écrits* (Paris: Editiones Franciscaines, 1953). Later he published *Sainte Claire d'Assise: documents, biographie, écrits, proces, et bulle de canonisation, textes de chroniquers, textes legislatifs et tables* (Paris: Éditions Franciscaines, 1983).

[5] Marie-France Becker, Jean François Godet, and Thaddée Matura eds., *Claire d'Assise: Écrits*, Sources Chrétiennes (Paris: Les Editions du Cerf, 1985).

[6] *Écrits* 10, n. 1, cites *Écrits Francois d'Assise*, Sources Chrétiennes 285, (Paris: Les Editions du Cerf, 1985).

[7] *Écrits* 16, n. 17, cites these sources: J. Plachy, *Žiwot bl. Anežky* (W. Praze v Vurbana Goliásse, 1666) and *Acta Sanctorum*, (Antwerpen: Martii I, 1688), 506-08.

dinis Fratrum Minorum.[8] In more than four centuries since the publication of the Latin edition of the letters, translations have appeared by language groups in both the Eastern and Western worlds. In 1915 Walter Seton published a Middle German version of the four letters following a fourteenth-century manuscript found at Bamberg.[9] His work led him to conclude that the German text was not a translation of the Latin text of Clare's first letter, but a re-translation of a German text. This conclusion led him to search for the base text in Latin from which the medieval German translation had been made. Seton discovered that the base text he was attempting to find was preserved in Codex 10 of the Chapter Library of Saint Ambrose of Milan and had been retrieved several years earlier by Achille Ratti, the future Pope Pius XI, who served at that time as the prefect of the library.[10] In 1924 Walter Seton in *Archivum Franciscanum Historicum* published the Latin text of Clare's letters based upon the Milan manuscript.[11]

In 1932, J.K. Vyskôcil produced a definitive critical edition of the four letters to Agnes of Prague along with an edition of the life of Blessed Agnes, *Vita beatae Agnetis.*[12] Seton established the authenticity of the letters in determining that the Milan manuscript was copied at Prague between January 18 and November 8, 1332. Seton surmised that it was produced and sent to Rome in an effort to promote the canonization of Agnes.

---

[8] *Écrits* 16, n. 19, states that this manuscript is preserved at the Convent of the Friars Minor of Hall in Austria and described in *Analecta Franciscana* 111, Quaracchi 1897, xvi.

[9] *Écrits* 16, n. 20, identifies this text as Walter Seton, *Some New Sources for the Life of Blessed Agnes of Bohemia*, British Society of Franciscan Studies 7 (Aberdeen, 1915), 51-55 and 151-64.

[10] *Écrits* 17, n. 21, cited as A. Ratti, "Un codice pragense a Milano con testo inedtio della vita de S. Agnese di Praga," *Randiconti dell'Instituto Lombardo di Scienze e Lettere*, ser. 11, 29 (1896): 392-96.

[11] *Écrits* 17, n22 cites Walter Seton, "The Letters of Saint Clare to Blessed Agnes of Bohemia," *Archivum Franciscanum Historicum* 17 (1924): 509-19.

[12] J.K. Vyskôcil, *Legenda Blahoslavené Anežky a čtryi listy Sv. Kláry* (Prague, 1932); trans. into Italian by L. Barabas, "Le lettere di santa Chiara alle beata Agnese di Praga," in *Santa Chiara d' Assisi*, Studi e cronaca del VII Centenario 1253-1953, VII (Assisi, 1954): 123-43.

The first English translation of Clare's letters, the work of Ignatius Brady, appeared as the *Writings of Saint Clare of Assisi* to commemorate the 750th anniversary of her birth in 1953.

This was followed in 1982 by *Francis and Clare: The Complete Works*, edited and translated by Regis J. Armstrong and Brady in the Paulist Press series, Classics of Western Spirituality.

Clare's writings, and other documents pertaining to the Poor Ladies of San Damiano and Francis's brothers was published in 1988 as *Clare of Assisi: Early Documents*, edited and translated by Armstrong. This work was revised and expanded in 1993 for the celebration of Clare's eighth centenary, published by the Franciscan Institute as *Clare of Assisi: Early Documents*. The most reliable and complete translation of the letters and additional primary sources for the study of Clare's Letters is the 2006 updated, reorganized, and enhanced third edition of *Clare of Assisi: Early Documents*.

Since there is no reliable manuscript of Clare's two letters to Ermentrude, the Cologne Beguine who settled in Bruges, but only a summary of their content included in the *Annales Minorum*, Grau concludes that Wadding's text cannot be construed to be Clare's writing.[13] Nonetheless, the similarity of its content to Clare's four letters led to its inclusion as a supplementary text.

CLARE OF ASSISI (1193-1253)

As a noble woman in her early twenties, Clare left her home and began to follow the Gospel way of life undertaken by Francis. Daughter of Favarone d'Offreduccio, at an early age Clare began to pattern her life according to the values of her mother, Ortulana, a faith-filled woman who had made a pilgrimage to Jerusalem. Pregnant and faced with the fear of losing the life of her first child and her own life, she made a pilgrimage across the boot of Italy through the mountainous terrain to the shrine of Saint Michael at Mount Gargano. Sister Cecilia, who came to the monastery of San Damiano three years after Clare, testified that when Ortulana was praying there before the cross,

---

[13] *Écrits* 19-20, n. 27, cites Luke Wadding, *Annales Minorum*, ad Ann. 1257, suppl. 20 (Quaracchi, 1931), 90-91.

"she heard a voice that told her she would give birth to a great light which would illumine the world" (Proc 6.12).[14] As a young girl, Clare showed concern for the poor by saving part of her food for the hungry. Generous of heart, she knew of Francis and contributed some of her resources to help rebuild the Porticuncula, the favorite little plot where his first brothers gathered to live.

More than forty years later, Clare's youngest sister Beatrice recalled how Francis had come to visit Clare in her family home and how after that they had frequent conversations. According to the Legend of Saint Clare, on Palm Sunday night, Clare and a companion left her home in order to devote her life to penance.[15] Clare made a dramatic move, unpopular with her family who had planned for her marriage to a suitor who would add his patrimony and land to the Offreduccio household. Instead, Clare chose to turn her back on the privileges and wealth of her aristocratic status in order to identify more closely with the poor and the teaching of the gospel. Such an interior reversal, or conversion, was confirmed by an outward sign when Francis tonsured Clare's hair.

When Francis was tonsured, he received the right to preach publically as well as to consecrate women for the enclosed life. Clare and her sister Catherine, known as Agnes in religious life, were both dedicated to religion by Francis and began to live adjacent to the church of San Damiano which Francis had rebuilt in response to the call he heard to repair God's home. Clare and her sister Agnes were representative of women's religious movements of the thirteenth century described by the historian David Herlihy as a time of the "feminization of sanctity."[16] Soon other women began to dedicate their lives in the pursuit of holiness along with Clare and Agnes at San Damiano, including her younger sister Beatrice and her mother, Ortulana.

---

[14] The Acts of the Process of Canonization, held two months after Clare's death, records the testimonies of thirteen sisters who had lived with Clare and were interviewed under oath. Sister Cecilia di Gualtieri Cacciaguerra of Spoleto, the sixth witness, was one of the first companions of Clare. *Clare of Assisi: Early Documents*, ed. and trans., Regis J. Armstrong (New York: New City Press, 2006), 167-71. Hereafter cited as CA:ED.

[15] "The Legend of Saint Clare," CA:ED, 285-86.

[16] David Herlihy, *Medieval Households* (Cambridge: Harvard University Press, 1985), 127.

Beyond their personal desire to find a place where they could live in accord with the message of the gospel and to share its good news in word and deed, Clare and her sisters seem to have had only simple intentions. It was a way of life parallel to the one Francis and his brothers were beginning to pursue and it attracted followers in Assisi and its neighboring towns. As the brothers began to travel, stories of the sisters' life at San Damiano spread throughout Italy and beyond into Eastern Europe.

AGNES OF PRAGUE (1211-1282)

Agnes was raised in a family of royal women publicly known for the holiness of their lives, including her aunt Saint Hedwig of Silesia (1274-1243), and her cousin Elizabeth of Hungary (1207-1231).[17] At an early age Agnes, daughter of King Přemsyl Ottakar I and his second wife Queen Constance from the Hungarian Arpad dynasty, was sent to the court of the duke of Silesia to be educated in preparation for marriage to the duke's son.[18] Upon his death when she was still only three years old, she returned to Prague and was placed in a Premonstratentian convent to complete her education. Soon after in an arranged political alliance Agnes was betrothed to Henry, son of Emperor Frederick II, and sent to Austria. When Henry married Leopold's daughter, Agnes persuaded her father not to retaliate with military force. Later Ottokar received and refused requests for Agnes to marry King Henry of England and the Emperor Frederick II. Throughout this time, Agnes devoted herself to charitable works in Prague. Meanwhile, when Francis's brothers came to Prague in 1225,

---

[17] See the biography of Agnes in Joan Mueller, *Clare's Letters to Agnes: Texts and Sources* (St. Bonaventure, NY: The Franciscan Institute, 2001), 5-11.

[18] CA:ED 39. This brief summary of Agnes's life follows Armstrong. The first biography in the English-speaking world was written to commemorate the seventh centenary of Clare's death: Nesta deRobeck, *St. Clare of Assisi* (Milwaukee: Bruce, 1951). In 1989 Marco Bartoli wrote *Chiara d'Assisi* which was translated into English and published in 1993 by Franciscan Press, Quincy, Illinois, along with two English studies written for the eighth centenary of her birth: Ingrid J. Peterson, *Clare of Assisi: A Biographical Study*, and Margaret Carney, *The First Franciscan Woman*. Since that time many reliable studies about Clare, her writings, and her spirituality have been produced in English and others have been translated into English.

Agnes built a church for them. No doubt through her contact with them, Agnes learned of Clare and the foundation of Poor Ladies at San Damiano. She obtained land through her brother and built a hospice for the sick of Prague, a monastery for women to follow the Gospel life in the manner of Clare, and a residence for the brothers who would minister to them. Then Agnes requested Pope Gregory IX's approval to request sisters from Clare's foundation at San Damiano in order to establish a similar foundation of Poor Ladies in Prague. In 1234, Agnes, seven other noble women from Bohemia, and five women from Assisi entered the new monastery.

Clare and Agnes both lived fully immersed in the cultural world of their times with its values shifting away from the class structure that, as a member of the aristocracy, had secured Clare's way of life in a culture hungry for profit and property often acquired through force or violence. Both women turned away from the privileges of their birthright and turned to Christ who could give them neither security nor status. Leaving one world, they established communal families modeled upon the humanity of Christ and his message. Unlike the hierarchical structures of medieval monastic women, Clare and Agnes sought a life that was grounded in equal respect for all. They practiced a leadership of service to one another and to the civic community that embraced them. What they taught by example took flesh as new members came to join them. Just as for Francis who declared that the Lord gave him some brothers, so were both Clare and Agnes given some sisters. The gospel message began to take root in the enclosed world of women.

Clare and Agnes were united in their realization that a papally approved form of life was imperative to preserve their way of poverty without common property. They stood together in their struggle to preserve what they referred to as "the privilege of poverty," that is, a papal exemption permitting them to receive women without dowries guaranteeing them a lifetime of support. Agnes was key in this effort and capitalized upon her royal status and the need of the papacy to strengthen its political position against the Holy Roman Empire by forming an alliance with the kingdom of Bohemia. Agnes's brother, King Wenceslaus, provided leverage in defense of his sister against Pope Gregory IX helping to bring the Form of Life they hoped for to fruition, forging a new papally-approved way for their monasteries and for women to live in the Franciscan tradition. The letters from Clare to Agnes indicate some of this struggle but, more importantly, they reveal the depth of her faith and her unflappable tenacity.

THE EPISTOLARY GENRE

Clare's letters represent the epistolary genre, for the most part the only genre accessible in her time for women's written expressions. Through letters, women throughout history were able to bypass the need for formal education, literary patronage, editors, publishers, and even the requirements of a patriarchal literary industry. Karen Cherewatuk and Ulrike Wiethaus contend that letters in which ideas and emotions are expressed directly provided women with an immediate audience.[19] Clare used her letters to establish and maintain communication, acknowledge Agnes's spiritual accomplishments, advise and instruct her in the practice of religious life, convey gratitude, and ultimately forge a deep spiritual bond. The finesse of Clare's letters make a distinctive contribution to the medieval genre of letter writing.

Because the Middle Ages was essentially an oral culture, the written word bestowed authority to both sender and receiver. Clare's letters to Agnes were no doubt read aloud to her community and widely circulated to other houses attempting to live without ownership of property, yet within the fold of the church. Letters were often written as quasi-public documents and even served as legal documents, as was true of papal correspondence. The public dimension of Clare's letters outweighs their private context. To read Clare's letters to Agnes with our modern notion of correspondence as an exchange between two persons is to misread their communal intention. The personal letter did not come into existence until the rise of vernacular languages. The strength of Clare's epistolary legacy is another indication that she did not remain muted by the prescriptions of her time. Nearly eight-hundred years later, we still hear her voice beyond the cultural and ecclesiastic controls of her time.

The rhetorical requirements of medieval times displayed complex strategies for an author to engage the audience. Because letter writing is dialogical, Agnes is present in Clare's letters, determining in part

---

[19] Karen Cherewatuk and Ulrike Wietaus, eds., *Dear Sister: Medieval Women and the Epistolary Genre* (Philadelphia: University of Pennsylvania Press, 1993), 1.

the form, content and the way Clare represents herself. When Clare describes her lowliness and humility, she employs the convention both classical and medieval authors used to place themselves in relationship to their audience. Clare identifies herself as an *ancilla*, a handmaid, in imitation of the Virgin Mary who called herself God's handmaid.

The *ars dictaminis*, or *ars dictandi*, the study and practice of epistolary composition, which originated in Italy lists the five parts of a letter which became standard in medieval Europe; the *salutatio* or greeting, which carefully articulated the recipient's social position; the *benvolentiae captatio* or means to enlist the good will of the recipient; the *narratio* or statement of purpose; the *petitio* or argument; and the *conclusio* or conclusion.[20] This format is developed from the divisions of classical oratory. Given that Clare was excluded from the schools in which the art of the epistolary genre was taught, it is not surprising that she followed the form only as a general guideline. Nonetheless, Clare's letters indicate considerable skill in applying these rules while adapting them to her needs.

Clare's letters are an incomplete record of her correspondence. Agnes's letters to Clare are obviously missing, and perhaps additional correspondence from Clare herself. It would seem unlikely that Clare's final address to Agnes, "to her who is half my soul," would spring from only a previous few interchanges. Cherewatuk and Wiethaus conclude the introduction to their study on the epistolary genre with this caution, "In analyzing the texts of medieval women writers, we assume that the corpus of surviving letters represent a fraction of what women originally wrote."[21]

II. Approaching the Text

Sources for the Study of the Letters

The most extensive full-length study of Clare's four letters is a work published in the Netherlands in 1994 by Edith Van den Goorbergh and Theodore Zweerman, translated into English in 2000 as *Light Shining*

---

[20] Cherewatuk and Wietaus, "Dear Sister," 5 n. 12, cite the manual of Alberic of Monte Casino.

[21] Cherewatuk and Wiethaus, "Dear Sister," 15.

Through a Veil: On Saint Clare's Letters to Saint Agnes of Prague.[22] The
intention of their study is to analyze the letters according to literary
schemata and concentric designs in the midst of the historical context
which shaped their writing. Thus, their method results in alternating
close textual criticism with expository sections. Van den Goorbergh
and Zweerman draw from the Biblical tradition, the ecclesiastical tradition, and the papal correspondence surrounding the letters in Appendix I.[23] Appendix II provides useful historical information relevant
to Clare's discussion of fasting in the Third Letter.[24] Their book makes
the Latin text readily available to English-speaking readers and provides an alternate translation of the letters to the Brady-Armstrong
translation in *Francis and Clare: The Complete Works* in the Paulist Press
series, Classics of Western Spirituality.

In 2001 Mueller's *Clare's Letters to Agnes: Texts and Sources* provided
yet another English translation of the four letters along with a study of
Agnes of Prague heavily documented with recent Czech studies. Mueller also supplies an English translation of *The Legend of Saint Agnes of
Rome*, as well as essays on Agnes's *Legend*, the relation of Clare's letters
to the early brothers, and the Privilege of Poverty as a source. This
translation was re-printed in Mueller's 2003 commentary, *Clare of Assisi: The Letters to Agnes*. Claire Marie Ledoux's reflections on Clare's
letters in French were translated as *Clare of Assisi: Her Spirituality Revealed in Her Letters* and published in 2003. Numerous other writings
on Clare draw from her letters. Francis Teresa Downing's *Living the
Incarnation* and *This Living Mirror: Reflections of Clare of Assisi* draw
heavily from the letters and provide practical applications from their
content for contemporary readers.

---

[22] Edith Van den Goorbergh and Theodore Zweerman, *Light Shining Through a
Veil: On Saint Clare's Letters to Saint Agnes of Prague*, trans. Aline Looman-Graaskamp
and Frances Teresa Downing (Leuven: Peeters, 2000); originally published as *Clara
van Assisi: Licht vanuit de verborgenheid*, Series Scripta Franciscana of the Franciscan
Study Centre Utrecht, vol. 2 (The Netherlands: Van Gorcum & Camp, 1994).

[23] Whereas Van den Goorbergh and Zweerman include headings in Chapter 1
indicating a discussion of the Biblical tradition on pages 78-80, and the ecclesiastical
tradition on pages 80-82, they make constant references to both traditions in explicat-
ing each letter. Appendix I includes a narrative on some of the papal correspondence
that may have precipitated Clare's second and third letters, 297-303.

[24] Van den Goorberg and Zweerman, *Light Shining*, Appendix II, 305-13.

Historical Context

The enormous public celebration in 1234 upon Agnes's dedication as a Poor Lady is the occasion of Clare's first extant letter. The passages taken from the liturgy of solemn consecration of virgins indicates that this letter was written for Agnes's passage from a life of wealth to her dedication to "God-centered poverty." Clare's second letter, written while Elias was general minister (1234-1239), encourages Agnes to persevere in her desire to live without property despite the difficulties she was encountering from the papacy. Clare's Third Letter is also a response to Agnes's request for advice regarding the Cistercian manner of fasting that was being imposed upon them. Both of these letters indicate the muddy ecclesiastical water which Clare and Agnes negotiated in beginning an untried way of religious living for women. Like her initial contact with Agnes, the Fourth Letter also appears to be initiated by Clare, who after years of mutual support, imparts to Agnes the hidden core of her contemplative journey to God.

New and revised translations of papal documents and Armstrong's introductory material on Pope Honorius III (1212-1222), Pope Gregory IX (1227-1241) and Innocent IV (1243-1253) included as Related Documents in the 2006 edition of *Clare of Assisi: Early Documents* under the rubric, "A Dossier for the Order of Saint Damien" provide a useful selection of primary sources to establish the context of Clare's letters from an ecclesiastic perspective.[25] The papal decrees can be interpreted either as positive efforts to regularize the developing women's communities within canonical prescriptions, or as an ecclesial means of power and control. The papal correspondence included in *Clare of Assisi: Early Documents* pertains to the issues that involved the juridical establishment and continuation of the monasteries, especially in Assisi and Prague.

Decrees under Pope Honorius III

The decrees beginning with Honorius III indicate papal efforts to envelop Clare and the various houses of Damianites within the juridical arms of the church, to assure their material support, and to

---

[25] Armstrong, CA:ED, 333-87.

protect them against charges of heresy. Honorius attempted to protect the legal ownership of their property as a means to guarantee their continuation. In order to accomplish his goal, Honorius established each house separately under the rule of Saint Benedict, granting to some the additional right to impose the "Regular Observance of the Ladies of Saint Mary of Saint Damian at Assisi."[26] The insistence that Agnes of Prague adhere to the papal prescriptions of ownership for enclosed women becomes a thorny issue about which she seeks Clare's advice. Clare's Second Letter counsels Agnes in this instance to skirt the uniform legislation regarding property and ownership in favor of the ideals of Francis and his brothers regarding poverty.[27]

Decrees under Pope Gregory IX

That the terms under which a religious house for women is founded cannot be amended continues to be a refrain throughout the reigns of Gregory IX and Innocent IV. The decrees of Gregory IX began to use the title "Order of Saint Damian" in referring to all the monasteries he was attempting to unite as one enclosed order under a single legal umbrella begun when he served, as Hugolino, as Cardinal Protector.[28] Gregory's 1234 correspondence to Agnes, *Sincerum animi*, written at the time of her religious dedication echoes the sentiments expressed by Clare in her first letter, including references to the early Christian martyr Agnes, the rejection of transitory things in favor of a heavenly Spouse, and Agnes's humility in choosing to be a handmaid instead of a queen.[29] In appointing Agnes as abbess, Gregory also grants her the faculty to exempt her sisters from some of the directives regarding fasting as prescribed in Benedict's Rule. His intervention in small

---

[26] Gregory IX, *Sacrasancta Romana Ecclesia*, December 9, 1219, in Armstrong, CA:ED, 337.

[27] Gregory IX, *Cum relicta*, May 18,1235, in Armstrong, CA:ED, 353-54.

[28] Armstrong, CA:ED, 333. The seminal article which began to unravel the distinction between Clare's Poor Ladies from Gregory's Order of San Damian is Maria Pia Alberzoni, "San Damiano in 1228: A Contribution to the Clare Question," *Greyfriars Review* 13.1 (1999): 105-23. For a developed treatment of her work see the English translation of Maria Pia Alberzoni, *Clare of Assisi and the Poor Sisters in the Thirteenth Century* (Saint Bonaventure, NY: Franciscan Institute Publications, 2004).

[29] Gregory IX, *Sincerum animi*, August 30, 1234, in Armstrong, CA:ED, 351-52.

matters of religious observance crops up again in regard to fasting, as is evident from Clare's response to Agnes in the third letter.

Gregory's 1235, *Cum relicta saeculi*, addressed to Agnes and her sisters sets the stage for Clare's third letter. Gregory felt that the funds generated by the hospice could be used as support for the monastery. Accordingly, he issued this letter which lays bare the iron-fist with which the papacy dealt with the houses of religious women during this time.

> Because you, My daughter the Abbess, have constructed it on land of the Roman Church, We have considered it with all that belongs to it as perpetually submissive to that same monastery. Notwithstanding these prescriptions, the same hospice with all that belongs to it may not be separated from the monastery in any way or by any excuse.... It is not permitted for anyone to impinge upon this statement of Our decree or for anyone to impose.[30]

However, Gregory relinquished and retracted his decision in April 1238 through his decree, *Pia credulitate tenentes*, which allowed Agnes's monastery in Prague to renounce their hospice which permitted them to live in accord with the "poverty of the Queen of Virgins" who "did not have a place to go among the poor even when she gave birth to the King of heaven." Having provided his rationale for conceding to take a more lenient position, Gregory decrees:

> Hence, We accept your free renunciation of the Hospice of Saint Francis in the diocese of Prague together with its rights and pertinences, which was given to you at one time and through you to your monastery. Therefore, overcome by your petitions and tears, We grant by the authority of this letter that you cannot be unwillingly forced to accept any possessions from this time on.[31]

---

[30] Gregory IX, *Cum relicta saeculi*, May 18, 1235, in Armstrong, CA:ED, 354.

[31] Gregory IX, *Pia credulitate tenentes*, April 14, 1238, in Armstrong, CA:ED, 356.

Gregory's 1237 decree, *Licet velut ignis*, addressed to "all his daughters in Christ, the Abbesses and Sisters of the Order of Saint Damian," re-introduces his regulation about fasting in imitation of Cistercian practices. He wields his power with the verbal hammer of obedience threatening any community that deviates from his instruction:

> Therefore, by the foresaid authority We more strictly forbid and restrain anyone of you, whether Brother or Sister, except the infirm, the feeble, and girls who otherwise cannot observe the rigor of regular life because of their tender age, from eating meat within the enclosures of your Monasteries, nor may you even serve it to someone outside. We enjoin this on your whole community in virtue of obedience by firmly admonishing you in advance that if you do not wish to incur danger to your souls, you should take care to observe this inviolably.[32]

This communication presented problems for the monasteries of women who were living according to the precepts of Francis. The second part of Clare's Third Letter indicates how Clare advised Agnes to deal with the dilemma they faced along with the other monasteries established in the manner of Francis's way of gospel life.

The following month in May 1238 Gregory issued another harsh decree, *Angelis gaudium*, attempting to stifle her efforts to free herself from the Benedictine Rule in order to more closely follow the way of life adopted by Clare and her sisters at San Damiano. He explains to Agnes that Clare received a one-time-only exemption from Pope Honorius, granted when, as Hugolino, he served as Cardinal Protector:

> Surely, O daughter of benediction and grace, when We were yet established in a lesser office, and that beloved daughter in Christ, Clare, the Abbess of the Monastery of Saint Damian in Assisi, and certain other devout women in the Lord cast aside worldly vanity and chose to serve Him under the yoke of religious observance, Blessed Francis gave them, as new-born

---

[32] Gregory IX, *Licet velut ignis*, February 9, 1237, in Armstrong, CA:ED, 354-55.

children, not solid food but rather a milk drink, a formula of life, which seemed to be suited for them.[33]

Furthermore, Gregory argues that because of this exemption, Clare never followed Francis's *Form of Life*, since her monastery was established under Benedict's *Rule*, and that Benedict's *Rule* is to be uniformly observed everywhere during his reign. In short, Agnes's monastery was professed under Benedict's *Rule* and that

> whatever zealous action may perhaps be suggested to you by someone not having sufficient knowledge, the most important consideration should be whether it is pleasing to God, acceptable to Us and salutary for you and your community."[34]

Finally, Gregory exempts Agnes from following Francis's *Form of Life* and, with the dignity of papal rhetoric, adds that he doesn't want to hear any more about Clare and how she is following Francis's *Form of Life*:

> You are in no way held to that Rule [Francis's 'formula'] since it has not been approved by the Apostolic See. It is not observed by the oft-mentioned Clare, her sisters, or by others. What more can be said? One does not seem to violate a vow who changes it into something better. We absolve you and your Sisters from the observance of the formula according to the fullness of power conferred upon Us by the Lord.[35]

Decrees under Pope Innocent IV

Although in 1247 Pope Innocent IV revised the *Form of Life* issued by Gregory as Hugolino, he followed the stance taken by Pope Gregory that monasteries remain under the rule by which they were established, that it be an approved rule, and that efforts continue to regularize women's houses. Issued universally to all houses of women religious on November 13, 1247, *Quoties a nobis* reiterates that the Or-

---

[33] Gregory IX, *Angelis gaudium*, May 11, 1238, in Armstrong, CA:ED, 360-61.

[34] *Angelis gaudium*, in Armstrong, CA:ED, 361.

[35] *Angelis gaudium* in Armstrong, CA:ED, 362.

der of Saint Damian with its Benedictine *Rule* is the only way to re-solve the disparity between religious houses with various exemptions, dispensations, and rules.[36] The recent writings of Maria Pia Alberzoni, Lezlie Knox, and Joan Mueller delve into the heart-wrenching diffi-culties these and similar papal pronouncements created for Clare and Agnes in their attempts to live a way of life grounded on gospel values rather than on juridical legislation.

Questions of dating and authorship

In 1980 Grau determined that the First Letter was written before June 11, 1234, the date of Agnes's entry into the monastery, for Clare addresses Agnes as "the daughter of the king of Bohemia."[37] The Sec-ond Letter was written between 1234-1239 since there is a reference to Elias as minister general. Grau argues the Third Letter dates to early 1238 when Clare asked Gregory IX for a new Rule that was not based on the Benedictine Rule, but instead honored her desire not to own common property and to be guaranteed the ministry of the friars. The Fourth Letter was written in 1253 after the return of Clare's sister Agnes to San Damiano and before her death on August 11. Despite Grau's certitude, controversy remains around the dating of Clare's let-ters.

Questions also remain about the authorship of the four letters. In a 2004 issue of *Franciscan Studies*, Timothy J. Johnson argues that with-in the context of the community in which it was produced, Leo may have been a contributing author to Clare's letters.[38] Johnson begins by delineating Bonaventure's distinction of the roles of scribe, compiler, commentator and author in the composition of a text.[39] He explains that a scribe copies what is written by someone else without changing anything, whereas a compiler adds something additional to an author's original work. A commentator writes what belongs to someone else,

---

[36] *Quoties a nobis*, August 23, 1247, in Armstrong, CA:ED, 376-77.

[37] *Écrits* 18, n. 25, citing Englebert Grau, "Die Schriften der heilligen Klara und die Werkeihrer Biographen," *Movimento religioso femminile e francesanesimo nel secolo XIII* (Assisi, 1980), 201-02.

[38] Timothy Johnson, "Clare, Leo, and the Authorship of the Fourth Letter to Agnes of Prague," *Franciscan Studies* 62 (2004): 91-100.

[39] Johnson, "Clare, Leo and the Authorship," 91, n1.

but clarifies the original writing by subordinating his own writing to another text. An author places original writing in the forefront, but adds the writing of others as confirmation.

Applying Bonaventure's distinctions to his close textual examination of Clare's Fourth Letter, Johnson raises three related questions: 1) Who was Clare's scribe? 2) Who introduced her to the formal art of writing, and 3) Who guided her theological development?[40] Johnson focuses on the evidence of a scribal hand in the Fourth Letter to Agnes of Prague, and following Attilio Bartoli Langeli suggests Leo's possible literary links to Clare.[41] In the Latin texts of Clare's Fourth Letter, verses 35 and 36, the phrase *hoc inquit*, which would be translated as "she says," or "she said," does not appear in the English, Italian, French or German translations.[42] Yet this phrase was commonly inserted parenthetically by scribes to quote the speaker. Johnson turns next to "Concerning True and Perfect Joy," one of the "dictated writings" of Francis where the term *inquit* once again emerges.[43] Because Leo served as the scribe who wrote what Francis dictated without adding his own material, Johnson wonders if he might have served a similar role for Clare at San Damiano.[44] Leo exhibited secretarial ability, a long relationship with Francis, and proximity to Assisi. Leo had a much longer relationship with Clare than he did with Francis.

---

[40] Johnson, "Clare, Leo and the Authorship," 92.

[41] Johnson, "Clare, Leo and the Authorship," 91, cites Attilio Bartoli.Langeli, "Gli Autografi di frate Francesco e di frate Leo," (Turnout: Brepols, 2000).

[42] Johnson, "Clare, Leo and the Authorship," 93, n1, refers to Alfonso Marini, "*Ancilla Christi: plantula* sancti Francisci." *Gli scritti di Santa Chiara e la Regola, in Clara di Assisi.* Atte del XX Convengo internazionale, ed. Enrico Menesto (Spoleto: Centro italiano di studi sull'alto medievo, 1993): 128.

[43] Johnson, "Clare, Leo and the Authorship," 96. Evidence of a scribe or secretary also appears in the English translation of Clare's "Form of Life," Chapter One, where reference is made to Clare in the third person. "And, just as at the beginning of her conversion, together with her sisters she promised obedience to the Blessed Francis, so now she promises to observe the same inviolably to his successors. And the other sisters shall always be obliged to obey the successors of Blessed Francis and Sister Clare and the other abbesses canonically elected who succeed her (FLCl 1:4-5)." In Chapter Two and the remainder of the *Form of Life* Clare writes in the first person plural, translated as "us" and "we." However, at the heart of her *Form of Life* in Chapter Six, Clare writes in the first person singular when she refers to how "I, together with my sisters, willingly promised" obedience to Francis (FLCl 6:1).

[44] Johnson, "Clare, Leo and the Authorship," 97.

Although Leo or someone else assisted Clare, Emore Paoli argues in the introduction to the 1977 *Fontes Francescani* that their differing styles suggest that one scribe worked in some way in producing the letters of Clare and another one with the Form of Life, Testament, and Blessing.[45] Langeli's work examining Francis's handwriting, and the early accounts of Francis and his brothers equipped him to recognize the distinctive narrative voice of Leo in telling the Francis story.[46] Langeli suggests that Leo, after Francis's death in 1226, may have served as Clare's secretary. For during the years in which the four letters were composed Clare and her sisters, along with the Angelo and Rufino, developed great intimacy in order to preserve the gospel life of Francis.[47]

An alternate position is given in Leonhard Lehmann's lengthy study, "La questione del Testmant di s. Chiara," published in 2004, demonstrating the similarity of content in the Letters to Agnes and the *Testament*.[48] Their style is different in that the *Testament* reflects the spoken words, but the letters are elegant and embellished with classical rhetorical strategies. Lehmann concluded that whereas Leo may have been the redactor of the unrefined *Testament*, the intricate style of Clare's letters indicates they were redacted with the help of someone from the papal curia. Lehmann contends that Clare could readily have obtained help from the learned bishops of Assisi, Crescentius of Jesi (1247-1250) or Niccolo of Calvi (1250-1273).

An earlier analysis of Clare's letters by Mario Marti describes their elaborate style, including the use of classical rhetorical figures and constructions, as well as the *cursus* employed by the Roman Curia.[49] Marti points to the sophistication in verses 7-11 of the first letter and the greeting of the second letter. These passages are developed so the

---

[45] Johnson, "Clare, Leo and the Authorship," 98, refers to Emore Paoli's conclusion in the introduction to the *Fontes Francescani* that Clare's writings were produced by two different redactors.

[46] Johnson's, "Clare, Leo and the Authorship," 91, citation of Langeli.

[47] Johnson, "Clare, Leo and the Authorship," 97, refers to Marini's hypothesis that perhaps Leo or another companion who was near Clare between 1234 and 1253 served as Clare's scribe.

[48] Leonhard Lehmann, "La Questione del Testamento di S. Chiara," *Convivium Assisiense* 6.1 (2004), 257-305.

[49] Mario Marti, *Ultimi contributi dal certo al vero, con bibliografia dell'autore* (Galatina, 1995), 5-18.

structure parallels the sound according to a traditional musical and rhythmic style. Given that Clare's rudimentary knowledge of Latin grammar would not have improved beyond her conversion, Marti concludes that working alone Clare would not have been able to bring forth the literary artistry of her letter. Marini (1993), Marti (1995), Boccali (2002), Lehmann (2003), Johnson (2004), and Michael Cusato (2006) all hold that an experienced writer assisted Clare in composing the letters, or as Cusato claims, "someone who had a rich scriptural and theological reservoir of images ..."[50]

Cusato presents another parallel in tracing the theme of *commercium* in the first letter, written in 1235, and in the Sacred Exchange, written between 1235 and 1238, suggesting that Clare collaborated with others as a part of a "textual community."[51] Both texts use the economic term commerce as a metaphor to express the relationship with God in which the things of the earth are exchanged for the kingdom of God. These texts restate Saint Paul's assertion, "For you know the grace of our Lord Jesus Christ, that being rich he was made poor for your sakes so that through his poverty you might become rich" (2Cor 8:9). In his conclusion, Cusato posits Caesar of Speyer, a key figure among Francis's companions of the 1230s, as author of the Sacred Exchange and the primary collaborator with Clare in the first letter to Agnes.[52]

III. INTERPRETING THE LETTERS

Structure of Clare's greetings to Agnes

Clare's letters are stylistically more sophisticated than those of Francis. They are all written in Latin, demonstrate considerable education, and a refined knowledge of liturgical and scriptural texts. However, even if Leo or someone from the papal curia could be established as a scribe, it is undisputed that Clare is the author, the voice in the

---

[50] Michael Cusato, "*Commercium*: From the Profane to the Sacred," *Francis of Assisi: History, Hagiography, and Hermeneutics in the Early Documents* (Hyde Park, NY: New City Press, 2004), 179-209.

[51] Cusato, "*Commercium*," 189, n19.

[52] Cusato, "*Commercium*," 193-94.

foreground of the letters. The basic structure of classical letter writing is most evident in the greetings of Clare's four letters. They reveal the development of their relationship throughout nearly twenty years of correspondence. In 1234, Clare approaches Agnes cognizant of the distance between them because of Agnes's royal status. Clare highlights Agnes's high position in the political world as "daughter of the most excellent and illustrious King of Bohemia" (1LAg1). In the following year after Agnes's dedication to God, Clare addresses her as "the daughter of the King of Kings, the servant of the Lord of lords, the most worthy spouse of Jesus Christ, and, therefore, the most noble Queen, Lady Agnes" (2LAg1). Clare recognizes the greater nobility of Agnes as a daughter of God and spouse of Jesus Christ within the heavenly realm.

In the third letter, Clare identifies with Agnes as her spiritual sister while noting that Agnes's father Ottokar I died and has been succeeded by her brother, Vaclav III, also referred to as Wenceslaus.[53] Clare begins, "To the lady most respected in Christ and the sister to be loved before all mortals, Agnes, sister of the illustrious King of Bohemia, but now the sister and the spouse of the Most High King of heaven" (3LAg 1). The intimacy between Clare and Agnes forged from their determination to cling to a new vision of religious life for women fostered their mutual affection. Mindful of her own approaching death and transformation to life everlasting, Clare greets Agnes,

> To her who is half of her soul and the special shrine of her heart's deepest love, to the illustrious Queen and Bride of the Lamb, the eternal King, to the Lady Agnes her most dear mother, and, of all the others, her favorite daughter (4LAg1).[54]

Clare describes her relationship to Agnes as it shifted from external affiliation to spiritual bonding. Throughout the four discourses Clare uses relational words – daughter, sister, spouse, bride – but in spiritual contexts. At the close of the Fourth Letter Clare places Agnes before

---

[53] CA:ED, 344; Mueller, *Clare's Letters*, 7.

[54] The abbreviations used for each letter are: 1LAg, *First Letter to Agnes of Prague;* 2LAg, *Second Letter to Agnes of Prague;* 3LAg, *Third Letter to Agnes of Prague;* and 4LAg, *Fourth Letter to Agnes of Prague.*

her as "her most dear mother," the one who nurtured what was most precious within Clare, her fidelity to God.

Van den Goorbergh and Zweerman see Clare's letters as the concentrated fruit of her meditation. Consequently, they suggest that her letters are structured as concentric themes framing one another in such a way that the beginning and endings of the sections correspond with each other. In this circular way, like meditation, Clare's letters

> form connections between the various mysteries of the faith, between these mysteries and our existence, between who Christ is as mediator and who we are (and hope to be enabled to become).[55]

Jesus Marie Bezunartea has described the theme of a three-fold journey to be the framework of each letter.[56] He outlines how Clare identifies a starting point, a path, and a goal. Other commentators have described different patterns within the letters. What cannot be argued is that Clare followed the structure of epistolary genre. Her greetings and message of good will to Agnes are strikingly evident. In each letter she identifies a purpose and substantiates her message frequently by drawing from the evidence of her experience. Clare's conclusions and warm communication of affection to Agnes and her sisters in Prague are unmistakable.

Themes and Images

In his head note for Clare's letters, Regis Armstrong suggests central themes for each letter while acknowledging that other related subjects are also introduced. He finds poverty as the core theme of the First Letter, perseverance as the theme of the Second Letter, enclosure along with her mission to the church as themes in the Third Letter, and contemplative prayer as the central topic of the Fourth Letter.[57]

---

[55] Van den Goorbergh and Zweerman, *Light Shining*, 29.

[56] Jesus Marie Bezunartea, "Clare of Assisi and the Discernment of Spirits," *Greyfriars Review* 8, Supplement (1994): 75-81.

[57] CA:ED, 40-43. See also Regis J. Armstrong, "Clare of Assisi, the Poor Ladies, and their Ecclesial Mission in the 'First Life' of Thomas of Celano," *Greyfriars Review* 5 (1991): 384-424.

Various commentators find differing spiritual insights in the Four Letters. In accord with Paul Ricoeur's theory of interpretation, any text is more than "talk writ down."[58] A text is different than oral discourse in that its interpretation involves both explanation and understanding. He argues that the real meaning of any writing "lies not behind the text but in front of it." Readers of any text make it their own by entering into it, and responding by appropriating meanings. Accordingly, Clare's letters hold a "surplus of meaning" accommodating a variety of readers.

The Mirror Image

The mirror – the medieval *speculum* – unquestionably holds a dominant symbolic place throughout Clare's four letters, as it did throughout the writing of the Middle Ages. Ritamary Bradley in "Backgrounds of the title 'Speculum' in Medieval Literature," traces the development of the *speculum* tradition illustrating the variations on the twofold meaning, "to show the world what it is and ... to point out what it should be."[59] She found that Gregory of Nyssa (c. 335-394) was one of the most prolific writers on the figurative meaning of *speculum*. He explained that the mirror of the soul is able to be turned toward the sensible or the superior world, meaning either toward temporal or heavenly things. Gregory held that lives of virtue reflect divine beauty, as a mirror makes the rays of the sun visible even though it is too bright to look upon directly. Each creature adorns itself with beauty proper to its rank, in a descending subordination, becoming kind of a mirror of a mirror.

Bradley identified a key text in Saint Augustine's commentary, *Ennaratio in psalmum 103*, in which he includes the Book of Scripture as the mirror of knowledge.[60] The mirror is a paragon of right living

---

[58] An interpretation of the Secular Franciscan Order's Rule of 1978 using Ricouer's theory appears in Robert M. Stewart, *"De illis qui faciunt penitentium;" The Rule of the Secular Franciscan Order:" Origins, Development, Interpretation* (Roma: Instituto Storico dei Cappiccini, 1991). The treatment of Riceour's method of interpretation is drawn from Stewart's Chapter Five, "Toward an Interpretation of the Rule of 1978," 321-64.

[59] Ritamary Bradley, "Background of the Title 'Speculum' in Medieval Literature," *Speculum* 29 (1954): 103.

[60] Bradley, "Background," 111.

when it is said that God's commands, whether read or recalled to memory, are seen as a mirror, with a reference to the man in Saint James Epistle who beheld his face in a mirror and went off forgetful of his state.

Saint Augustine provides another variation on the mirror as a paragon for holy living in his rule for religious women, which was later adapted for monks. His image of what the monk should be was circulated under the title *Speculum*. Augustine's text closed with this injunction, "That you may see yourself in this little book as in a mirror and may not neglect anything through forgetfulness, let it be read to you once a week." Following Augustine, St. Benedict makes a variety of applications of the mirror, such as following the tenets of Scripture and performing good works for others.

In the twelfth century, Hugh of Saint Victor, further elaborated on the metaphor of the mirror in commenting on the Rule of Saint Augustine. He recommended,

Therefore, it is prescribed that you read this book until you know it by heart ... and it is rightly called a mirror, for we see in it as in a mirror in what state we are, whether beautiful or deformed, just or unjust ...[61]

For Hugh of Saint Victor the Rule was a book reflecting God, in the same way as the Book of Scripture, the Book of Nature, or The Book of Life. The presence of God or God's will can be "read" in these books.

Van den Goorbergh and Zweerman hold that each of Clare's four letters is characterized by a unique metaphor. In the First Letter Clare uses the idea of exchange or commerce, a popular image for a time in which, because of the advent of the merchant class, the exchange of goods for money was becoming a common business practice.[62] At the time of her religious consecration, Clare praises Agnes because she

---

[61] "Expositio in Regulum Beati Augustini," *Patrologia Latina*, CLXXVI, 923 D0924 A; translation in Bradley, "Background," 111.

[62] See Dalarun on the use of exchange in the allegory of Lady Poverty, *The Sacred Exchange*, in Jacques Dalarun, *Francis of Assisi and the Feminine,"* (St. Bonaventure, NY: Franciscan Institute Publications, 2006),139. See also Joseph P. Chinnici, "Francis and

has rejected marriage to the illustrious Emperor and chosen instead "a spouse of a more noble stock" (1CAg7), and received "the hundred-fold instead of one" (1Ag 30). Agnes and before her Clare exchanged earthly things for heavenly ones.

In the second letter, Van den Goorbergh and Zweerman argue that since Clare begs Agnes to persevere despite the difficulties she has encountered from the papacy, the way or the journey is its central image. The Third Letter revolves around the theme of God's dwelling place as Clare imagines Jesus dwelling within the womb of the pregnant virgin as well as making a home within every human soul. Among other images found in the Fourth Letter, Van den Goorbergh and Zweerman claim the symbolism of the bride is the central metaphor. This letter, written as Clare faces eternal union with God in death, is couched in allusions to the spousal imagery of the *Song of Songs*, a biblical text popularized by Bernard of Clairvaux in the eleventh century.

The introduction to the *Écrits* notes that the language of Clare's writing is much more typical of the spirituality that was prominent in her time than is the writing of Francis. Francis tends to employ images from the liturgical and ecclesiastical texts of his prayer. Clare's images, on the other hand, are often more in accord with the affective expressions of her contemporaries, especially so since the writings of the twelfth-century Benedictine nuns of Helfta and others were widely circulated.[63]

Clare: the Vocation of Exchange," *Proceedings of the Annual Federation Council Conference*, August 20-22, 1987.

[63] The writings of the nuns of Helfta represent the largest single body of women's mystical writing in the twelfth century. Their major texts are Mechthild of Magdeburg's *Flowing Light of the Godhead*, Mechthild of Hackeborn's *The Book of Special Grace*, Gertrude the Great's *Spiritual Exercises* and *The Herald of Divine Love*, or the *Revelations*. Translations of modern editions of some of these works are available as *Gertrude the Great of Helfta: Spiritual Exercises*, trans. Gertrud Jaron Lewis and Jack Lewis (Kalamazoo: Cistercian Publications, 1989), *The Herald of God's Loving-Kindness*, Books I and II, *Gertrude the Great of Helfta*, trans. Alexandra Barratt (Kalamazoo: Cistercian Publications, 1991), and *Mechthild von Magdeburg: Flowing Light of the Divinity*, trans. Christine Mesch Galvani (New York: Garland Publishing, 1991). Recent translations and studies of medieval women mystics abound.

Message and Meaning

The First Letter

Clare's letters provide a rich source of her spirituality as well as of the beliefs and practices that characterize Franciscan spirituality today. In the first letter, Clare reflects on the meaning of a religious consecration (1LAg 3-7) in terms of choice. She points out what Agnes has given up: magnificence, honor, and worldly dignity which could have been hers through marriage to Frederick II, the Holy Roman Emperor. Agnes exchanged these temporal goods for poverty and bodily want. Virginity, a gift from God, continues to empower Agnes enriching her with virtue (1Ag8-11). Clare describes these spiritual benefits using images that reflect Agnes's royal upbringing: precious stones, priceless pearls, sparkling gems, and a golden crown of holiness.

The next section demonstrates how the poverty and virginity of the "Poor Crucified" freed him for service to others (1LAg 12–14). Clare counsels that the cross is a sign for Agnes that, poor and pure, she will become both strong and available for service to others. Then Clare addresses poverty directly with poetic invocations under three titles: "O blessed poverty," "O holy poverty," and "O God-centered poverty (1LAg 15–17)." Much in the way that Francis personifies Lady Poverty, Clare portrays poverty as embracing those who love her and bestowing eternal riches upon them. Poverty also performs actions, promising the kingdom of heaven and revealing eternal glory to those who desire her. In the third invocation, Clare praises poverty as the virtue "embraced before all else" by the Lord Jesus Christ since he came from heaven and became poor on earth.

Clare's reference to the cross as an example of poverty leads her to further reflection on the mysteries of the Redemption and the Incarnation as evidence of God's service (1LAg 19–24). This paragraph echoes Clare's previous guidance for Agnes to be faithful in her service. She creates images of the poor Jesus who was born poor, lived with "nowhere to lay his head," and in the end gave up his Spirit, "so that people who were very poor and needy, suffering excessive hunger of heavenly nourishment, may become rich in Him by possessing the kingdom of heaven." Mary who heard the Word of God, conceived, and gave birth to Jesus is held up as a model for Agnes.

The commitment made by Agnes will be full of temptations presented by the lure of temporal things and their encumbrance (1LAg 25-29). Clare provides Agnes with scriptural testimony that her promise to be poor will guide her through difficulties and into the kingdom of heaven. The essence of the First Letter is captured in this summary: "What a great and praiseworthy exchange to receive the hundredfold in place of one, and to possess a blessed eternal life" (1LAg 30). Clare's closing is a final admonition about Agnes's journey, "progressing from good to better, from virtue to virtue" to serve God and others (1LAg 31-35).

The Second Letter

Clare's Second Letter begins with a paragraph of praise and thanksgiving for God's gifts and graces, especially as they are evident in the perfection of Agnes's life (2LAg 6-11a). Clare refers once again to Agnes's conversion noting that she had "despised the splendor of an earthly kingdom, ... and held fast to the footprints of him to whom you merited to be joined in marriage." Clare struggles to provide Agnes with words from which she can "draw some consolation." Calling forth her experience beset by setbacks, Clare suggests to Agnes that she "always be mindful of your commitment like another Rachael always seeing your beginning." Clare directs Agnes to walk the path of life with joy and perseverance, despite its challenges and obstacles:

> What you hold, may you hold,
> What you do, may you do and not stop.
> But with swift pace, light step, unswerving feet,
> so that even your steps stir up no dust,
> may you go forward securely, joyfully and swiftly,
> on the path of prudent happiness,
> believing nothing, agreeing with nothing
> that would dissuade you from this commitment
> or would place a stumbling bock for you on the way,
> so that nothing prevents you from offering
> your vows to the most high in the perfection
> to which the spirit of the Lord has called you
>   (2LAg 11-14).

Having provided Agnes with spiritual advice, Clare addresses Agnes's inquiry giving her pastoral advice (2LAg 11b-17). Faced with a "stumbling block," Agnes is directed to follow the advice of Brother Elias, who has counseled her to respectfully ignore the advice of anyone else.[64] History fills in what is missing between Clare's lines to Agnes. Pope Gregory's 1235 decree, *Cum relicta saeculi* commanded Agnes to join her monastery with the hospice on the same property, thus assuring the Poor Ladies of Prague a guaranteed means of livelihood. The dilemma for Agnes and her sisters was that under such an arrangement it would be impossible for the monastery to live without common property, the privilege of poverty that was so dear to Clare as a means of imitating the poor Christ. As the number of brothers increased during Elias's term as Minister General, he resolved a similar conflict for the brothers by turning the ownership of their houses over to the papacy.[65] In this way, the brothers were technically living without ownership as Francis desired, yet they were able to adapt their needs to establish places of residence. However, Elias's solution clashed with the agenda of Gregory IX's Order of Saint Damian which insisted that women religious own sufficient property for their maintenance.

The model for ownership and poverty for Clare is the "poor virgin" and the "poor Christ" (2LAg 18-23). The remainder of the letter exhorts Agnes to follow Christ, made possible by prayer. Clare sketches the steps in her method of prayer, "gaze, consider, contemplate," which lead to the imitation of Christ.[66] Christ provides an example for

---

[64] For a thorough discussion of Elias's relationship to Clare, see Maria Pia Alberzoni, *Clare of Assisi and the Poor Sisters in the Thirteenth Century* (St. Bonaventure, NY: Franciscan Institute Publications, 2004), 124-26. See also Joan Mueller, *The Privilege of Poverty: Clare of Assisi, Agnes of Prague, and the Struggle for a Franciscan Rule for Women* (University Park, PA: Penn State Press, 2006).

[65] Michael Cusato suggests the brothers employed a "legal fiction" to practice their vow of poverty while having the deed for the property in which they lived held by a second party. For example, the papacy owned the property on which Gregory IX built the Basilica of Saint Francis.

In refusing to own common property, Agnes and Clare, were attempting to trust only in God's providence for their maintenance. He treats this thorny issue for both the sisters and the brothers in "Elias and Clare: An Enigmatic Relationship," *Clare of Assisi: Investigations*, Clare Centenary Series, vol. 7 (St. Bonaventure, NY: The Franciscan Institute, 1993): 95-115.

[66] For a discussion of Clare's techniques of prayer, see Timothy J. Johnson, "Visual Imagery and Contemplation in Clare of Assisi's 'Letters to Agnes of Prague',"

Agnes in his suffering in that he became lowly, despised, was struck, scourged, and died on the cross. Clare reminds Agnes that suffering will lead to glory for her, as it brought Christ to resurrection. Once again Clare juxtaposes the transitory earthly journey against the glory of heaven, and perishable goods against everlasting glory.

The Third Letter

Clare's Third Letter is structured in two separate parts with two different purposes. In the beginning section, Clare shares her spiritual insights about Mary as an exemplar while in the second section she responds to Agnes's question about the practice of the monastery regarding the ascetical discipline of fasting. After an embellished greeting, Clare recounts the work God has accomplished through Agnes both spiritually and externally in becoming a "co-worker of God." Rejoicing in Agnes's achievements, Clare encourages Agnes to view her situation as an affirmation of her trials (3LAg 5-10). Agnes appears to be overtaken with discouragement in her efforts to establish a monastery the way she had envisioned it (3LAg11-16). Clare suggests a method of conversion, a way to climb beyond self-pity. Clare advises Agnes to stay positive, "always rejoice in the Lord;" to avoid negativity, "And may neither bitterness nor a cloud overwhelm you ..." Clare also recommends that Agnes try some new steps in her relationship to God in prayer, "Place your mind in the mirror of eternity! Place your soul in the figure of eternal glory! Place your heart in the figure of the divine substance." Finally Clare tells Agnes to anticipate changes in her disposition and transformation into the image of God, tasting God's "hidden sweetness" for her present discouragement will "completely pass away." Clare describes a movement from bitterness to sweetness, such as that experienced by Francis through his embrace of the leper.

For Clare, loving God begins with wonder at his coming into this world through the mystery of the Incarnation. Accordingly, the last part of the spiritual section of this letter presents the role of Mary's motherhood and its meaning (3LAg11-29). Clare portrays Mary, pregnant with the Word of God "in the little cloister of her holy womb."

Mystics Quarterly 19.4 (1993): 161-72; and "To Her Who is Half her Soul": Clare of Assisi and the Medieval Epistolary Tradition," *Magistra*, 2.1 (1996): 24-50.

Then she visualizes Jesus as an infant, holding him "on her virginal lap." The humility of God overwhelms Clare when she considers that while heaven could not contain the greatness of God, Mary was able to provide a dwelling place for God within her body. It is a further wonder that each soul is also a dwelling place of God. All humans, like Mary also carry within them the God who created them. Clare marvels that Mary and every soul fashions a home and throne for God.[67] Clare's conclusion reiterates that possessing the life of God-within-us is of indescribable value in contrast to any other transitory possession.

Having conveyed her reasons for gratitude, at this point in the Third Letter Clare turns to Agnes's questions regarding the Cistercian practice of fasting (3LAg30-41). Clare responds beginning, "Now concerning those matters you wished me to clarify for you ..." Clare advises that the poor Ladies at the Monastery of San Damiano are guided by the fasting customs of Francis and his brothers. However, Clare cautions,

> But our flesh is not bronze, nor is our strength that of stone, rather we are frail and inclined to every bodily weakness.... And I beg you in the Lord to praise the Lord by your very life, to offer the Lord your reasonable service and your sacrifice always seasoned with salt.

Such practical matters are wrapped in Clare's larger vision of the sacredness of each person, the *leit motif* of this letter. Clare views Agnes's discouragement about Gregory IX's fasting requirements imposed by his 1237 decree, *Licet velut ignis*, of small impact when considered against the dignity given by God to every person.

---

[67] Marco Bartoli, *Clare of Assisi*, trans. Frances Teresa Downing (Quincy, IL: Franciscan Press, 1993), 128-31, relates the Marian spirituality and spiritual motherhood to the theme of mystical marriage in Clare's first and fourth letters. Bartoli, 130, argues that, like Francis, Clare associates Mary with poverty, as the poor woman, the mother of the poor Jesus. Clare's Form of Life portrays Mary, wrapping herself in swaddling clothes, as a model of poverty for her sisters: "Out of love for the most holy and beloved Child wrapped in poor little swaddling clothes and placed in a manger, and of his holy mother, I admonish, beg and encourage my sisters always to wear poor garments" (FlCl 2:24).

The Fourth Letter

The Fourth Letter, written shortly before Clare's death, reviews the life, death, and glory of Jesus' return to God. After expressing regret for not writing more frequently, Clare reminds Agnes, whose name is derived from the Latin word for lamb, that she is "espoused to the spotless lamb who takes away the sins of the world." Throughout the entire letter she speaks in mystical language associated with heaven and the glory of resurrection. She represents heaven with terms of renewal and refreshment.

Clare's first long passage is a song depicting the vision of God (4LAg9-14). The heaven Clare anticipates is a sumptuous wedding feast, a "sacred banquet," in which "all the blessed hosts of heaven" and "all the citizens of the heavenly Jerusalem" are gathered to admire and reflect the glory of God shining from the face of Christ.[68] Christ is the "mirror without blemish" who reveals who God is, the visible sign of the invisible God.

Following Clare's designation of Christ as the mirror of God, she directs her words to Agnes who, in turn, is a mirror of Christ (4LAg15-23). Agnes is urged to prepare for union with God by adorning herself as for a wedding clothed with flowers and "all the virtues as is becoming the daughter and dearest bride of the Most High King." The virtues specific to Christ's story, poverty, humility, and charity, convey the story of his Incarnation, Redemption, death and Resurrection. Clare represents these virtues through the image of a medieval mirror with three distinct levels of clarity. Clare associates poverty with the birth of Christ, placing it at the border of the mirror. The surface of the mirror correlates with the humility of Christ's "untold burdens and punishments" throughout his life. The clearest point of the mirror at its center, or depth, identified as charity recalls the events of Christ's suffering and shameful death on the cross. This path, approached through gazing using the external senses, meditating using the faculties of the mind, and loving using the affections of the heart is the way Clare found to imitate and become united with Christ.

The following diagram maps out the intricacy of Clare's understanding of the relationship between the kinds of prayer and the cor-

---

[68] Dalarun, *Francis of Assisi and the Feminine*, 157.

responding parts of the mirror, the virtues, the mysteries of Christ's birth and passion, and the soul's progressive development:

Prayer ———►	Mirror ———►	Virtues ———►	Soul's Progress
Gaze	Border ———►	Poverty ———► Incarnation	Beginning
Consider ———►	Surface ———►	Humility ———► Passion	Middle
Contemplate ———►	Depth ———►	Charity ———► Suffering/Death	End

In the last major section of the fourth letter, Clare lifts the veil of her mystical life disclosing to Agnes how she has attained union with God (4LAg24-32). She indicates that she heard the invitation to follow the way of the cross by praying before it. Clare spent forty years of her life at the church of San Damiano with the cross that spoke to Francis. As Clare was pursued by God, she, in turn, directs Agnes to desire union with God. Clare describes her mystical experience drawing from the spousal imagery of Saint Bernard of Clairvaux and his commentaries on the Biblical *Song of Songs*.[69] Following Bernard, Clare represents the stages of the spiritual journey by using metaphors of feet for the beginning, or purgation of vices, hands for the middle, or illumination by acquiring virtue, and the kiss on the mouth which indicates union with God. The Incarnation has been described as the kiss of heaven and earth, of humanity and divinity.

Her instruction on contemplation and transformation complete, Clare exhorts Agnes to rest in the contemplation of God. Clare closes by reiterating her affection for Agnes of Prague and her sisters in the monastery. Her final words add the greetings of her blood sister, Agnes, who has returned to Assisi from the Monastery in Monticelli near Florence to keep vigil with Clare, her sisters, and all the sisters and brothers who surrounded Clare at the time of her death.[70]

---

[69] Jacques Dalarun, *Francis of Assisi and the Feminine*, 113, notes that Francis never uses the *Song of Songs* whereas Clare makes references to it seven times.

[70] Refer to the "Letter of Agnes of Assisi to her Sister Clare," CA:ED, 404-05.

CONCLUSION

Marco Bartoli and others have explored a theology of Clare, while others have claimed that Clare ought to be viewed as a vernacular theologian.[71] Bartoli asserts that because of the occasional nature of Clare's writings, it is not possible to construct a theology of Clare.[72] On the other hand, he argues that it is possible to distill her reflections of faith from her writings. He points to the passage from Clare's Testament in which the vocation of the Poor Ladies at San Damiano is described using the image of the mirror:

> For the Lord himself has placed us as a model, as an example and mirror not only for others, but also for our sisters whom the Lord has called to our way of life as well, that they in turn might be a mirror and example for those living in the world (TestCl 30).

Both reflecting on and reflecting the person of Jesus were core to Clare's spirituality. Her life of contemplation on the Christ crucified on the cross brought her to do what she could to relieve the suffering of other humans, and in so doing to minister to the God who was in her midst.

The spirituality of Clare centered on the poor and crucified Christ revealed through her letters records a first-person account of her inner journey. Because her experience of God is not edited by another hand, the letters present an authentic self-portrait of Clare's life in God. In contrast, *The Versified Legend of the Virgin Clare of Assisi* and *The Legend of Saint Clare*, documents composed previous to or surrounding the time of her canonization in 1255, are stories about Clare often based on the eye witnesses who knew her and whose testimonies are recorded in *The Acts of the Process of Canonization*.[73] The *Legend*, in particular, commissioned by Pope Gregory IX, features Clare as a model for his project to centralize for women the emerging forms of religious life under the rubric, the Order of San Damiano.[74] The form

---

[71] Marco Bartoli, Chapter 6, "The Theology of Prayer" in *Clare of Assisi*, 117-31.

[72] Bartoli, *Clare of Assisi*, 117.

[73] Translations of these documents are available in CA:ED.

[74] See Maria Pia Alberzoni, *Clare of Assisi and the Poor Sisters in the Thirteenth Century*, for a book-length treatment of Clare's Form of Life and Gregory's Order of

of life fostered by Gregory followed the Rule of Saint Benedict and did not incorporate the two values that were non-negotiable for Clare: the privilege of poverty which permitted houses to exist without common property, and the right of the sisters to benefit from the ministry and preaching of Francis's brothers.

It is important to realize that the Clare of the Letters is not the Clare of the *Legend*. Legends – biographical genre intended to be proclaimed aloud as readings for the office – functioned as didactic tools to inspire their hearers by the saintliness and miracles of their subject. The Clare of the *Legend* relates biographical facts and events that contributed to her holiness and elaborated on her miraculous interventions. Because Clare's healing acts are framed in the *Legend* by her devotion to the cross, Bartoli argues that the author is primarily interested in presenting his theology which may reach beyond that of Clare.[75] Margaret Carney's study points to Chapter VI of Clare's *Form of Life* which places poverty as its center.[76] Subsequent biographers to our day continue to reinterpret Clare's letters adding their own understanding.

Clare's letters reveal a spiritual depth rooted in contemplation focused on the poor Jesus and his poor mother. In praying before the image of the crucified Christ, Clare experienced the human face of God manifest as poverty, humility, and excessive charity. Her first two letters praise God for all the goodness that has been given to her, but especially for her vocation. Attentive to her quest for personal spiritual growth, Clare's prayer is centered on her spirituality and that of Agnes of Prague. The third and fourth letters indicate Clare's spiritual maturity as her prayer shifts from praise to wonder, not at what God does, but on who God is and how her life and that of Agnes achieve worth in the quest for God. Clare's letters testify how she remained loyal to the movement of the Spirit of God working within her soul. She translated

---

San Damian, as well as her earlier studies, "'Nequaquam a Christi sequla in perpetuum absolvo desidero' [I Will Never Desire in Any Way to be Absolved from the Following of Christ] Clare Between Charism and Institution," *Greyfriars Review* 12 (1999 Supplement): 81-121, and "San Damiano in 1228: A Contribution to the Clare Question," *Greyfriars Review* 13.1 (1999): 105-23.

[75] Bartoli, *Clare of Assisi*, 61.

[76] Margaret Carney, *Clare of Assisi: The First Franciscan Woman* (Quincy, IL: Franciscan Press, 1993).

the call of God into her voice, a voice she would not permit to be silenced by papal efforts to reconfigure the lives of enclosed women into one universal model. Clinging to her desire to live poor, like the poor Jesus and his mother, the letters reveal the strength Clare drew upon from her life of prayer. The hierarchy of the church failed to grasp her effort to live the Gospel in the manner of Francis and his brothers in their primitive experience of community life. The letters hint how the political fortification of Agnes of Prague's royal status provided help for each of them to negotiate a papally approved Form of Life. Together they succeeded in stretching the church to make a new place for women while remaining faithful.

Although not continuous in the time of their writing, these four letters reveal elements about Clare's spiritual journey and experience of God. They point out that Clare's starting point was her response to the call of God, the source of "every good and perfect gift (LAg 2:3)." Her journey began, as did that of Francis, by following in the footprints of the poor Christ. While many difficulties were encountered along Clare's way, fidelity to contemplation and to the *Form of Life* she envisioned for herself brought about her transformation. Adorned with the virtues of poverty, humility and charity, Clare had confidence she would be eternally united with and in God. In this way, as the human Jesus is a mirror of the invisible God, so Clare understood herself to be a mirror of Jesus Christ in the glory of the great God.

IV. BIBLIOGRAPHY

Manuscripts

Ambrosiana Library, (Milan), Iv, 4 f. 442 [17th cent.]

Herzogl. Bibliothek, (Helmstadt) Wolfenbüttel ms. Codex 132 [14th cent.]

Königl. Bilbiothek, (Berlin) ms. Germ. Oct 484. [14th cent.]

Königl. Bilbiothek, (Berlin) Dresden ms. M 281 [14th cent.]

Legenda Latina Sanctae Clarae Virginis Assisiensis. Introductione, testo restaurato, note, e indici a cura di P. Giovanni Boccali. Traduzione Italiana di Marino Bigaroni. Santa Maria degli Angeli: Edizioni Porzuncola, 2001.

Royal Library of Bamberg. Ms. Misc. History E. VII. 19, ff 139r-157v [14th cent.]

Royal Library of Bamberg. Ms. Misc. History E. VII. 54 [14th cent.]

Santa Chiara di Assisi: *I primi documenti ufficiali di canonizzazione.* Introduzione, testo, note, traduzione italiana dei testi latini e indici a cura di P. Giovanni Boccali. Santa Maria degli Angeli: Edizioni Porziuncola, 2002.

Translations

Claire d'Assise: Écrits. Introduction, Texte Latin, Traduction, Notes et Index. Eds. and trans. Marie-France Becker, Jean-François Godet, et Thaddée Matura. Paris: Les Éditions du Cerf, 1985.

Clare and Francis: The Complete Works. Ed. and trans. Regis J. Armstrong and Ignatius Brady. Classics of Western Spirituality. New York: Paulist Press, 1982.

Clare of Assisi: Early Documents. Ed. and trans. Regis J. Armstrong. New York: Paulist Press, 1988.

Clare of Assisi: Early Documents, rev. and exp. Ed. and trans. Regis J. Armstrong. St. Bonaventure, NY: Franciscan Institute Publications, 1993.

Clare of Assisi: Early Documents, rev. Ed. and trans. Regis J. Armstrong. New City Press, 2006.

Escritos de Santa Clara y documentos Contemporáneos, 2nd ed. Madrid: Biblioteca de Autores Cristianos, 1982.

Fontes Francescani. Ed. Enrico Menesto and Stefano Brufani. Santa Maria degli Angeli: Edizioni Porziuncula, 1995.

Sainte Claire d'Assise. Documents. Ed. Damien Vorreux. Paris: Editions franciscaines, 1983.

Writings of Saint Clare of Assisi. Trans. Ignatius Brady. St. Bonaventure, NY: The Franciscan Institute, 1953.

Complete English translations of the four letters also appear in the two studies listed below by Mueller and in the study by Van den Goorbergh and Zweerman.

Studies and Related Works

Alberzoni, Maria Pia. Clare of *Assisi and the Poor Sisters in the Thirteenth Century.* Saint Bonaventure, NY: Franciscan Institute Publications, 2004.

_____. "Clare of Assisi and Women's Franciscanism." *Greyfriars Review* 17:1 (2003): 5-38.

_____. "Nequaquam a Christi sequela in perpetuum absolvo desidero" [I Will Never Desire in Any Way to be Absolved from the Following of Christ] Clare Between Charism and Institution. *Greyfriars Review* 12 (1999 Supplement): 81-121.

_____. "San Damiano in 1228: A Contribution to the Clare Question." *Greyfriars Review* 13.1 (1999): 105-23.

Armstrong, Regis J. "Clare of Assisi: the Mirror Mystic." *The Cord* 35 (1985): 81-121.

_____. "Clare of Assisi, the Poor Ladies, and their Ecclesial Mission in the 'First Life' of Thomas of Celano." *Greyfriars Review* 5 (1991): 384-424.

_____. "Starting Points: Images of Women in the Letters of Clare."*Greyfriars Review* 7.3 (1991): 347-80.

Bartoli, Marco. *Clare of Assisi.* Trans. Frances Teresa Downing. Quincy, IL: Franciscan Press, 1993.

_____. *Chiara: una Donna tra Silenzio e Memoria.* Torino: Edizioni San Paolo, 2001.

Beha, Marie. "Praying with Clare of Assisi." *The Cord* 57.4 (1997): 185-93.

Bezunartea, Jesus Marie, "Clare of Assisi and the Discernment of Spirits." *Greyfriars Review* 8. Supplement (1994).

Borkowski, Mark. "Two Medieval German Translations of the Letters of St. Clare of Assisi." Diss. Chapel Hill, NC, 1954.

Brunelli, Delir. "Contemplation in the Following of Jesus Christ: The Experience of Clare of Assisi." *The Cord* (2002): 154-70.

Carney, Margaret. *Clare of Assisi: The First Franciscan Woman*. Quincy, IL: Franciscan Press, 1993; St. Bonaventure, NY: Franciscan Institute Publications, 2007.

Cherewatuk, Karen and Ulrike Wiethaus, eds. *Dear Sister: Medieval Women and the Epistolary Genre*. Philadelphia: University of Pennsylvania Press, 1993.

Chinnici, Joseph P. "Francis and Clare: the Vocation of Exchange." *Proceedings of the Annual Federation Council Conference*, August 20-22, 1987.

Cronica XXIV Generalium Ministrorum Ordinis Fratrum minorem 1209-1374. *Analecta Franciscana* 3. (Quarrachi: Collegii S. Bonaventurae, 1897) 184-86.

Cusato, Michael, "Commercium: From the Profane to the Sacred," *Francis of Assisi: History, Hagiography, and Hermeneutics in the Early Documents*. Hyde Park, NY: New City Press, 2004. 179-209.

Dalarun, Jacques. *Francis of Assisi and the Feminine*. St. Bonaventure, NY: Franciscan Institute Publications, 2006.

Delio, Ilia, "Identity and Contemplation in Clare of Assisi's Writings." *Journal of Studies in Spirituality* 14 (2001): 139-52.

_____. "Mirrors and Footprints: Metaphors of Relationships in Clare of Assisi's Writings," *Laurentium* 41 (2000): 454-71.

"De sanctae Clarae Virginis." *Acta Sanctorum* II. Paris, 1897.

Doyle, Eric. "Discipleship of Christ in St. Clare's Letters to Blessed Agnes of Prague." *Franciscan Christology: Selected Texts*. Translations, and Introductory Essays. Ed. Damian McElrath. St. Bonaventure, NY: The Franciscan Institute, 14-39.

Resource Manual for the Study of Franciscan Christology. Ed. Kathleen Moffatt. Washington, DC. Franciscan Federation, 1998. 381-85. Reprint from *Franciscan Christology: Selected Texts*. Translations, and Introductory Essays. Ed. Damian McElrath. St. Bonaventure, NY: The Franciscan Institute.

Dozzi, Dino. "Chiara e Specchio." In *Chiara: Francescanesimo al Femminile*. Ed. Davide Covi and Dino Dozzi. Roma: Edizioni Dehoniane, 1992). 290-318.

Fasbinder, Maria. "Untersuchungen über die Quellen zum Leban der hl.Klara von Assisi. *Franziskanische Studien* 3 (1936): 297-300.

Flanagan, Eileen. "Medieval Epistolary Genre and the Letters to Agnes of Prague." *Spirit and Life* 11 (2004): 51-53.

_____. "Rediscovery of the Poor Clare Tradition in Clare of Assisi's *Letters to Agnes of Prague*." Unpublished dissertation. Temple University, 2000.

Godet, Jean François. "A New Look at Clare's Gospel Plan of Life." *Greyfriars Review* 5. Supplement (1991) 1-84.

Godet-Calogeras, Jean François and Roberta McKelvie, eds. *An Unencumbered Heart: A Tribute to Clare of Assisi*. Spirit and Life 11: A Journal of Contemporary Franciscanism. St. Bonaventure, NY: Franciscan Institute Publications, 2004.

Grau, Engelbert, ed. *Leben und Schriften der heligen*, Klara von Assisi. Werl/Westfalen: Dietrich-Coelde Verlag, 1988. 22-24.

Hammond, Jay. "Clare's Influence on Bonaventure?" *Franciscan Studies* 62 (2004): 101-17.

Hammond, Jay, ed. *Francis of Assisi, History, Hagiography and Hermeneutics in the Early Documents*. Hyde Park: New City Press, 2004. 39-63.

Hardick, Lothar. *La spiritualita di S. Chiara: Commento del'vita agli scritti della Santa*. Milan: Edizioni Biblioteca Francescana, 1986.

Hone, Mary Frances. *Toward the Discovery of Clare of Assisi: Clare Centenary Series*. 8 volumes. St. Bonaventure, NY: Franciscan Institute, 1992-1995.

Introduccion a Santa Clara de Asis. Curso de Santa Clara por correspondencia. Zaragoza, Spain: Universidad de Zaragoza, 1980-81. [The letters are analyzed by J.M. Castro, F. Aizpurua and A. Amunarriz.]

John Paul, Pope. "Canonization of Agnes of Bohemia and Albert Chmielowski." *Greyfriars Review* 4.1 (1990): 143-49.

Johnson, Timothy J. "Clare, Leo, and the Authorship of the Fourth Letter to Agnes of Prague." *Franciscan Studies* 62 (2004): 91-100.

_____."Images and Vision: Contemplation as Visual Perception in Clare of Assisi's Epistolary Writings." *Greyfriars Review* 8.2 (1994): 201-17. Reprinted from *Collectanea Franciscana* 64 (1994): 195-213.

_____."To Her Who is Half her Soul: Clare of Assisi and the Medieval Epistolary Tradition." *Magistra*, 2.1 (1996): 24-50.

_____. "Visual Imagery and Contemplation in Clare of Assisi's 'Letters to Agnes of Prague'." *Mystics Quarterly* 19.4 (1993): 161-72.

Karper, Karen. "The Mirror Image in Clare of Assisi." *Review for Religious* 51 (1992): 424-31.

Langeli, Attilio Bartoli. "Gli Autografi di frate Francesco e di frate Leo." Turnout: Brepols, 2000.

Ledoux, Claire Marie. *Clare of Assisi; Her Spirituality Revealed in Her Letters*. Trans. Colete Joly Dees. Cincinnati: St. Anthony Messenger Press, 2003.

Lehmann, Leonhard. "La Questione del Testamento di S. Chiara." Published as *Convivium Assisiense*. Assisi: Edizioni porziuncola, 2003. 257-305.

López, Sebastián. "Lectura teológica de la Carta I de santa Clara." *Selecciones de Franciscanismo* 19 (1990): 14-32.

_____. "Lectura teológica de la Carta II de santa Clara." *Selecciones de Franciscanismo* 20 (1991): 299-320.

_____. "Lectura teológica de la Carta III de santa Clara." *Selecciones de Franciscanismo* 22 (1993): 418-35.

_____. "Lectura teológica de la Carta IV de santa Clara." *Selecciones de Franciscanismo* 23 (1994): 258-74.

Lynn, Beth, "Early Friars and the Poor Ladies in Conversation: *Scripta Leonis* and the Writings of Clare: A Common Matrix of Evangelical Contemplative Life for both Men and Women." *The Cord* 45.1 (1995): 21-30.

McGinn, Bernard. *The Flowering of Mysticism; Men and Women in the New Mysticism 1200-1350; The Presence of God: A History of Western Christian Mysticism.* Vol 3. New York: Crossroad, 1998.

Marini, Alfonso. "'Ancilla Christi: plantula sancti Francisci': Gli scritti di Santa Chiara e la Regola," *Chiara di Assisi*. Atte del XX Convengo internazionale. Ed. Enrico Menesto. Spoleto: Centro Italiano di studi sull'Alto Medievo, 1993. 107-56.

Marti, Mario. *Ultimi contributi dal certo al vero, con bibliografia dell'Autore.* Galatina: Congedo Editore, 1995. 5-18.

Miller, Ramona, and Ingrid Peterson. *Praying With Clare of Assisi.* Companions for the Journey Series. Winona, MN: Saint Mary's Press, 1994.

Mooney, Catherine M. *"Imitatio Christi* or *Imitatio Mariae?"* Clare of Assisi and her Interpreters." In *Gendered Voices: Medieval Saints and their Interpreters.* Ed. Catherine M. Mooney. Philadelphia: University of Pennsylvania Press, 1999. 52-57.

Mueller, Joan. *Clare of Assisi: The Letters to Agnes.* The Liturgical Press: Collegeville, MN, 2003.

_____. *Clare's Letters to Agnes: Texts and Sources.* St. Bonaventure, NY. The Franciscan Institute, 2001.

_____. *The Privilege of Poverty: Clare of Assisi, Agnes of Prague, and the Struggle for a Franciscan Rule for Women.* University Park, PA: Penn State Press, 2006.

Peterson, Ingrid J., ed. *Clare of Assisi A Biographical Study.* Quincy, IL: Franciscan Press, 1993.

_____. "Clare of Assisi: Espoused to the Crucified." *A Leaf from the Great Tree of God: Essays in Honour of Ritamary Bradley.* Toronto: Peregrina Publishing, 1994. 156-72.

_____. "Clare of Assisi: Hidden Behind Which Image of Francis?" Ed. Jay Hammond, *Francis of Assisi, History, Hagiography and Hermeneutics in the Early Documents.* Hyde Park: New City Press, 2004. 39-63.

_____. *Clarefest Selected Papers: Clare of Assisi: A Medieval and Modern Woman.* Vol. 8. Clare Centenary Series. St. Bonaventure, NY: Franciscan Institute, 1995.

Polc, Haroslav. *Agnes of Boehmen 1211-1282: Konistochter-Aebissin-Heilige.* Angelus Waldenstein Wartenburg München: R. Oldenbourg Verlag, 1989.

Poor Clares of the Holy Name Federation and the Mother Bentivoglio Federation. *Doing What is Ours to Do: A Clarian Theology of Life.* St. Bonaventure, NY: Franciscan Institute, 2000.

Purfield, Brian. "Reflections in the Mirror: the Images of Christ in the Spiritual Life of Saint Clare of Assisi." Master's thesis. St. Bonaventure, N.Y.: Franciscan Institute, 1990.

Ratti, Achille. "Un codice pragense a Milano cone testo inedito della vita di S. Agnese di Praga." *Rendiconti dell'Istuto Lombardo di Scienze e Lettere II* 29 (1896): 392-96.

Raurell, Frederic. "La Lettura del 'Cantico dei Cantici' al tempo di Chiara e la 'IV lettera ad Agnese di Praga'." *Laurentianum* 31 (1990): 198-309.

Schlosser, Marianne. "Mother, Sister, Bride: The Spirituality of Clare." *Greyfriars Review* 5.2 (1991): 233-49.

Schmidt, Margot. "Miroir." *Dictionnaire de spiritualité ascétique et mystique doctrine et historoire*. Vol. 10. 1290-1303.

Seton, Walter W. "The Letters of St. Clare to Blessed Agnes of Bohemia." *Archivum Franciscanum Historicum* 17 (1924): 509-19.

St. Clare of Assisi and Her Order: A Bibliographic Guide. Ed. Mary Francis Hone. Clare Centenary Series. Vol 5. St. Bonaventure University: The Franciscan Institute, 1995.

Triviño, Maria-Victoria. "El gozo de Clara de Asis en su primera carta a Inés de Praga." *Selecciones de Franciscanismo* 10 (1981): 198-309.

_____."El Cantar de los Cantares en la Carta de Santa Clara de Asis." *Selecciones de Franciscanismo* 11 (1982): 25-31.

Van Assoldonk, Optatus. "The Holy Spirit in the Writings and Life of Clare." *Greyfriars Review* 1.1 (1987): 94-104.

Van den Goorbergh, Edith, O.S.C. "Clare's Prayer as Spiritual Journey." *Greyfriars Review* 10.1 (1996): 283-92.

Van den Goorbergh, Edith, and Theodore H. Zweerman. *Light Shining Through a Veil: On Saint Clare's Letters to Saint Agnes of Prague*. Trans. Aline Looman-Graaskamp and Frances Teresa Downing. Leuven: Peeters, 2000. Originally published as *Clara von Assisi: Licht vanuit de verborgenheid*. Vol. 2 in the Series Scripta Franciscana of the Franciscan Study Centre. Utrecht, The Netherlands, 1994.

Vyskočil, Jan Kapistran. *Legenda Blahoslavené Anyžky a čtyri listy. Sv. Kláry*. Prague: Nakladatelsvi Universum, 1932. 90-93.

Vyskočil, Jan Kapistran and Leo Brabas. "Le letere di Santa Chiara alla Beata Agnese di Praga." *Santa Chiara d'Assisi: Studi e cronaca del Vii centenario 1253-1953*. Assisi: Comitato Centrale per il VII Centenario 1253-1953 Morte S. Chiara, (1953).

The *Form of Life* of the Poor Ladies

Lezlie Knox

Introduction

With the bull *Solet annuere*, issued on August 9, 1253, Pope Innocent IV approved Clare of Assisi's *forma vitae*.[1] Clare had begun the work of composing her form of life – her rule – several years earlier, only after the pope reluctantly admitted that his new legislation for the enclosed women attached to the Order of Lesser Brothers had failed to win their support. As a result of this decision, the sisters would not be required to profess it.[2] This concession opened a new opportunity for Clare to advocate a distinct way of life for her community. She emphasized that the sisters were to live without material endowments, and be sustained solely on alms and pastoral ministry from the Friars Minor.

For almost three decades Clare had resisted ecclesiastical efforts to regularize San Damiano by consistently seeking exemptions that confirmed their commitment to radical poverty. Now, with *Solet annuere*, Clare appeared to have secured a permanent endorsement for the sisters' life of radical poverty. Sister Filippa, speaking later to the papal investigators examining the cause for Clare's canonization, identified

---

[1] I have used Clare's own term *forma vitae* (form of life, abbreviated FLCl) when talking specifically about the text she authored in the middle of the thirteenth century. The attribution *Rule of Saint Clare* refers more generally to the reputation it developed over time.

[2] See *Bullarii Franciscani Epitome sive summa bullarium in eiusdem bullarii quattuor prioribus tomis relatorum, addition supplement*, ed. C. Eubel (Florence: Quaracchi, 1908), 249.

the confirmation of the rule as the triumphant culmination of her abbess' struggle.

> At the end of her life, after calling together all of her sisters,
> she entrusted the *Privilege of Poverty* to them. Her great desire
> was to have the *Form of Life* of the Order confirmed with a pa-
> pal bull, to be able one day to place her lips on the papal seal,
> and, then, on the following day, to die. It occurred just as she
> desired. She learned a brother had come with letters bearing
> the papal bull. She reverently took it even though she was very
> close to death and pressed that seal to her mouth in order to
> kiss it. On the following day, Lady Clare passed from this life
> to the Lord – truly clear without a stain, with no darkness of
> sin, to the clarity of eternal light.[3]

Clearly the rule's approval was very important to Filippa and the
other sisters at San Damiano. Thus it is perhaps surprising that there
is no direct reference to Clare's *forma vitae* in either the bull of canonization or the hagiographical legends produced by the Roman curia (c.
1254-1255).[4] The *vitae* focus simply on Pope Innocent's deathbed visit
to bless Clare and then later recount her death two days later in the
company of the sisters and several friars.[5] This silence also extends to

---

[3] Sr. Filippa was a witness at Clare's canonization process, see PC 3:32. I have
used the standard English translation of this text; *Clare of Assisi: The Lady*, ed. Regis
Armstrong (New York: New City Press, 2006), 162.

[4] Although Sr. Filippa's testimony uniquely refers to the confirmation of the rule,
this silence does not indicate the other sisters' lack of interest. The entire community
(except for the sisters in the infirmary) was likely present during the questioning as
their testimonies only briefly overlap and seem concerned to present a full picture of
Clare. Moreover, the notaries may have truncated testimonies as one example shows,
namely, Sr. Angeluccia's recollection of Clare's Trinitarian visions. When asked what
else the abbess had said, the notary recorded "... she replied as Sister Filippa had previously (PC 14:7)." It is not clear if the notary was being economical to avoid record-
ing the same testimony, or whether Angeluccia herself had briefly confirmed Filippa's
lengthier account of the final days of Clare's life. Sister Christiana's reference to Clare
"reminding the sisters of the perfect observance of the Order" also may be a veiled
reference to Clare's *forma vitae*, see PC 13:10.

[5] Compare VLCl 31-32 and LCl 41-42. The medieval *Vita Innocenti IV* also overlooks the approval of Clare's rule. This biography is published in Alberto Melloni,
Innocenzo IV: La concezione e l'esperienza della cristianità come regimen unius personae (Ge-
noa: Marietti, 1990), 259-93. The description of his visit (actually two visits) to Clare
comes on 285.

visual representations of Clare. For example, the "Assisi Retable," the earliest panel painting featuring a cycle of scenes from her life, similarly excludes any image of the papal confirmation of her rule.[6] The lack of reference to her *forma vitae* in these sources reflects Clare's transformation into a generic model of female sanctity deemed appropriate for cloistered women: enclosed, silent, and penitential.[7] Additionally, such omission indicates the problematic status of her *forma vitae*. The ecclesiastical hierarchy, unlike her sisters, was not interested in calling attention to Clare as author of a rule that promoted radical poverty; indeed, Pope Innocent IV explicitly granted approval of her *forma vitae* to her own community of San Damiano alone.[8] Nevertheless, scholars now identify Clare of Assisi as the first woman to compose a monastic rule for other religious women.[9] This designation makes a powerful

---

[6] This panel has been dated to between 1281-1285. See Jeryldene Wood, *Women, Art and Spirituality: The Poor Clares of Early Modern Italy* (Cambridge: Cambridge University Press, 1996), 11-33.

[7] Marco Bartoli suggests that there was an intentional suppression of her rule by the author of the *Legend of Saint Clare*, see his *Chiara d'Assisi* (Rome: Istituto Storico dei Cappuccini, 1989), 236 note 44 [English translation, *Clare of Assisi*, trans. Sister Frances Teresa (Quincy, IL: Franciscan Press, 1993), 235 note 44. Clare's hagiographic transformation has received more attention from Italian scholars, for example Giovanna La Grasta, "La canonizzazione di Chiara," in *Chiara d'Assisi: Atti del XX Convegno, Assisi, 15-17 ottobre 1992* (Spoleto: Centro Italiano di Studi sull'Alto Medioevo, 1993), 301-24. However, see now Miles Pattenden, "The Canonisation of Clare of Assisi and Early Franciscan History," *Journal of Ecclesiastical History* 59 (2008): 208-26.

[8] *Solet annuere* concludes ... *vobis omnibus vobis que in vestro monasterio succedentibus in perpetuum confirmamus* ["... we confirm forever for all of you and for all who succeed you in your monastery"].

[9] This identification gained currency from Thaddée Matura's introductory essay in *Claire d'Assise: Écrits*, ed. Marie-France Becker, Jean François Godet, and Thaddée Matura, *Sources Chrétiennes* 325 (Paris: Éditions du Cerf, 1985), 41. Examples of this oft repeated epithet include Elizabeth Alvilda Petroff, "A Medieval Woman's Utopian Vision: The Rule of Clare of Assisi," in her collection *Body and Soul: Essays on Medieval Women and Mysticism* (Oxford: Oxford University Press, 1994), 66-67 and Nancy Bradley Warren, *Spiritual Economies: Female Monasticism in Later Medieval England* (Philadelphia: University of Pennsylvania Press, 2001), 25. This tendency is not limited to Anglophone scholarship. Leonhard Lehmann observed "Per chi voglia studiare le donne nel medioevo, infatti, sarebbe impossibile prescindere dall'unica donna che ha lasciato un testo legislative da lei composto per altre donne, come appunto fu la Regola di Chiara." ["In fact, for those who would study women during the Middle Ages, it would be impossible to overlook the sole woman who has left a legislative document composed by herself for other women, as is the case with the Rule of Clare.] "Le Fonti Francescane Nuova Edizione (2004): Osservazione e Valutazione," *Archivum Franciscanum Historicum* 99 (2006): 319.

claim for her importance in the larger history of medieval women. Clare appears to represent what other contemporary religious women lacked: a strong female voice which not only campaigned for their spiritual ideals, but also provided an institutional form for them.[10]

Although her *forma vitae* dates from the final years of her life and is her sole piece of legislative writing, it strongly influences how historians have chosen to write about Clare's life. Many scholars locate her significance in the struggle to secure the right for women to live without endowments in the face of significant opposition from masculine authorities, including both the ecclesiastical hierarchy and the Lesser Brothers themselves.[11] Some have also seen the rule as representing Clare's efforts to shape female Franciscan institutions. This assertion draws upon a pious tradition from the later Middle Ages that recognized her as founder of an enclosed order of Franciscan nuns.[12] However, this popular image overstates the immediate institutional impact of the *Rule of Saint Clare* by presenting Clare as founder of the female Franciscan Order.

Certainly, her *forma vitae* offers important testimony to Clare's fidelity to Francis's spiritual ideas and her efforts to shape community life at San Damiano. But although a few other communities sought permission to adopt it, most Poor Ladies were not attracted to its

---

[10] While Clare's *forma vitae* was the earliest female-authored rule to receive papal approval, this representation overlooks other contemporary women authors of religious rules. The most important of these was Isabella of France, whose monastic legislation is discussed by Sean Field in a future volume of this series. Dominican sisters also collaborated on rules, see Maiju Lehmijokii-Gardner, "Writing Religious Rules as an Interactive Process: Dominican Penitent Women and the Making of Their *Regula*," *Speculum* 79 (2004): 660-87.

[11] Jo Ann Kay McNamara features Clare in a chapter entitled "Disordered Women," in *Sisters in Arms: Catholic Nuns through Two Millennia* (Cambridge: Harvard University Press, 1996), 304-12. Joan Mueller's recent monograph also incorporates Agnes of Prague into this struggle: *The Privilege of Poverty: Clare of Assisi, Agnes of Prague and the Struggle for a Franciscan Rule for Women* (University Park, PA: Pennsylvania State University Press, 2006). Mueller's focus allows her to complicate the usual narrative that juxtaposes the brief triumph of Innocent's approval with the rapid suppression of Clare's *forma vitae*. An example of this arc is Patricia Ranft, "An Overturned Victory: Clare of Assisi and the Thirteenth Church [sic]," *Journal of Medieval History* 17 (1991): 123-34.

[12] For example, a recent encyclopedia on medieval women directs readers to the entry for "Clare of Assisi, St." when they look up "Poor Clares." See *Women in the Middle Ages: An Encyclopedia*, ed. Katharina Wilson and Nadia Margolis (Westport, CN: Greenwood Publishers, 2004), specifically vol. 2, 761.

model of radical poverty and did not want it to govern their houses.[13] Furthermore, her rule remained unfamiliar to most Franciscans – both the sisters and the brothers – during the later thirteenth and fourteenth centuries. In parts of France and throughout England, most sisters professed a rule composed by the royal princess Isabelle of France (1259; revised 1263).[14] Most Italian communities of the Poor Ladies came to adopt Pope Urban IV's constitution issued on October 18, 1263.[15] This bull formally instituted the Order of Saint Clare leading to the historical irony that its members – who we can only refer to as Clarisses or Poor Clares after this date – professed the "Urbanist" rule, not the *Rule of Saint Clare*. It was not until the fifteenth-century movement which became known as the Regular Observance that widespread interest in Clare's *forma vitae* was reborn. Reformers identified it as the "first rule" (*prima regula*). The historical significance of the *Rule of Saint Clare* thus resides not only in its thirteenth-century origins in the community at San Damiano, but also in its rediscovery and revival as a part of later reform movements. The complex history of its transmission, combined with its variable authority, has much to say about the status of Clare of Assisi herself within the Franciscan tradition.

I. Establishing the Text

Two manuscripts have proven especially important for establishing the text of the *Rule of Saint Clare*. The first of these is a parchment, preserved among Clare's relics in the Protomonastery in Assisi, which has been identified as the earliest known copy of the rule. It provided the basis for the first critical edition published in *Seraphicus legislationis tex-*

---

[13] For use of the term Poor Ladies to refer to the female poverty movement, see an example in 1C 18. Since the 1230s, the sisters had been known as the Order of San Damiano or Damianites. This confederation had grown out of a complex variety of spiritual ideals and forms of life that were only somewhat unified by papal attempts to regularize women's life. Clare's relationship to the Damianite Order is discussed below in the section on Historical Context.

[14] The later, revised rule is published in *Bullarium Franciscanum* II, 477-86. See Sean Field, *Isabelle of France: Capetian Sanctity and Franciscan Identity in the Thirteenth Century* (Notre Dame: University of Notre Dame Press, 2006), 61-120 esp.

[15] *Bullarium Franciscanum* II, 509-21.

tus originales in 1897,[16] as well as subsequent versions.[17] The date of the other manuscript, the famous Messina codex, has been the subject of much debate concerning its origin and date. This codex too remains in the possession of the Clarisses, preserved at the library of the convent of Montevergine in Sicily. Together these two manuscripts raise important questions about the structure and transmission of Clare's *forma vitae*. Moreover, recent codicological research on both documents has begun to change in significant ways what has long been the common understanding of the manuscript tradition of her rule.[18]

The rediscovery of the Assisi manuscript in 1893 laid the groundwork for modern appreciation of the *Rule of Saint Clare*. When her tomb was opened to mark the seven hundredth anniversary of Clare's birth, a parchment containing the bull of approbation, *Solet annuere*, which includes the text of her *forma vitae*, was discovered in a reliquary box within the folds of her habit.[19] An unidentified hand recorded in the margins that "the blessed Clare touched and kissed this many times out of her devotion (*hanc beata Clare tetigit et obsculata [sic] est pro devotione pluribus vicinis*)."[20] This note was not written at the time of Clare's

---

[16] Hilaire de Paris, *Seraphicus legislationis textus originales* (Quaracchi: Collegio di San Bonaventura, 1897). Two years earlier, Giuseppe Cozza-Luzi had published photographs of the manuscript; "Un autografo di Innocenzo IV e memorie di Chiara d'Assisi," *Pontificia Accademia Romana di Archaeologia* 4 (1895): 50-55.

[17] These more recent editions also made use of five other Latin manuscripts of Clare's rule which primarily date from the later Middle Ages (including the Messina codex). These manuscripts are discussed briefly in the following text and are listed in the bibliography. The editions are: *Regula et Constitutiones generales pro monialibus Ordinis Sanctae Clarae* (Rome: Tipografia Poliglotta "Cuore di Maria," 1930; revised in 1941 and 1973); Giovanni Boccali, *Opuscula s. Francisci et scripta s. Clarae Assiensium* (Assisi: Biblioteca Francescana, 1978); and *Claire d'Assise: Écrits* in *Sources Chrétiennes*, which is now the standard edition to which most scholars refer. Nonetheless, the 1995 compilation *Fontes Franciscani* reprints the Boccali edition.

[18] An overview of these findings is addressed below, but see also at greater length, Federazione S. Chiara d Assisi delle Clarisse du Umbria-Sardegna, *Il Vangelo come forma di vita: In ascolto di Chiara nella sua Regola* (Padua: Messagero di Sant'Antonio Etrice, 2005), 21-70.

[19] For a description of its discovery, see *Seraphicus legislationis textus*, 2-3. Clare's tomb had already been opened and relics removed in 1850 and 1864, but the small box containing the rule does not seem to have been opened at either time. See Mary Clare, "The Finding of the Body of Saint Clare, September 23, 1850," *The Cord* 35 (1985): 247-53.

[20] For the notes on the document, see Paschal Robinson, "Inventarium omnium documentorum quae in Archivio protomonasterii S. Clarae Assisiensis nunc asserva-

death, but seems to have been added during an inventory conducted in the first decades of the fourteenth century, drawing on community tradition and perhaps a record of the canonization process with Sister Filippa's testimony.[21] Two other notes on the manuscript were identified as papal autographs, thus confirming its authenticity and status as the original text of the *Rule of Saint Clare* for most scholars.[22] In the upper left margin, Pope Innocent IV wrote *Ad instar fiat!* – so be it! – and signed the initial *S* for Sinibaldus, his birth name. Below, a slightly longer note added "for reasons known to me and to the protector of this convent, so be it (*ex causis manifestis michi et protectorii mon[asterii] fiat ad instar*)."[23] This comment has been interpreted as a reference to the rushed circumstances under which Pope Innocent IV first orally confirmed the rule on Clare's deathbed. After he returned to his residence in Perugia, the papal chancery issued *Solet annuere* to secure its juridical status. This bull unusually includes the complete text of Cardinal Rainaldo de' Segni's own confirmation of Clare's *forma vitae*, *Quia vos*, dating from September 16, 1252. Its incorporation reflects the obvious urgency under which the chancery needed to proceed. But it also raises the question of how much involvement Rainaldo had in the drafting of the rule, a point which is addressed to a greater extent below.

---

tur," *Archivum Franciscanum Historicum* 1 (1908): 417. Cozza-Luzi also transcribed the notes, reading "dicta" rather than "beata."

[21] Comparison with other bulls in the convent archives containing notes in a similar hand suggest that it was placed there during an archival inventory taken between 1323-1343. See Federazione S. Chiara d Assisi delle Clarisse du Umbria-Sardegna, *Chiara di Assisi: Una vita prende forma. Iter storico* (Padua: Messaggero di Sant'Antonio Editrice, 2005), 117 note 15.

[22] The somewhat "miraculous" rediscovery of this document raised some suspicions initially; see for example, Edmund Wauer, *Entstehung und Ausbreitung des Klarissenordens besonders in Deutschen Minoritenprovinzen* (Leipzig: J.C. Hinrichs, 1906). Most scholars since have accepted its historicity, hence this story of the rediscovery is repeated in each of the editions and translations. Maria Pia Alberzoni's decade-old call for a critical reexamination of the papal signatures has only just occurred as this essay discusses shortly. See her *Chiara e il Papato* (Milan: Edizioni Biblioteca Francescana, 1995), 103 note 175. [English translation, "Clare and the Papacy," in *Clare of Assisi and the Poor Sisters in the Thirteenth Century* (St. Bonaventure, NY: Franciscan Institute Publications, 2004), 85 note 175.]

[23] These translations appear in Armstrong, *The Lady*, 106-07. Cozza-Luzi's transcription differed: "ex causis mihi et protectori fiat ad instar." These differences reflect the difficulty inherent in reading the faded text.

Due to the presumed papal autograph, the Assisi manuscript regularly is identified as the original text of both the *Rule of Saint Clare* and *Solet annuere*. It is striking, though, that the structure of the former's text is unique among medieval manuscripts of her rule. The text is continuous without any division into chapters or even titles indicated with rubrics or other means such as initial letters.[24] The other medieval manuscripts all incorporate such partitions. Therefore, two questions must be asked about the transmission of Clare's *forma vitae*: is the Assisi parchment really the "original" text, and when was it divided into chapters and by whom. The Messina manuscript suggests answers to both of these questions.[25]

This small codex has long been identified as one of the key sources for understanding the transmission of Clare's writings.[26] In addition to the *Rule of Saint Clare* and *Solet annuere*, it contains the 1216 *Privilege of Poverty* attributed to Pope Innocent III, as well as her writings whose authenticity have long been questioned – her *Testament* and *Benediction*. Most scholars had identified the manuscript as a central Italian production which could be dated to no earlier than the second half of the fourteenth century and, more likely, from the mid-fifteenth century. Perhaps it was taken to Sicily by friars on a preaching tour, where it eventually came into the possession of the Observant sisters at Montevergine, founded in 1464 by Eustochia Calafato. A late medieval date was supported by Werner Maleczek who studied the manuscript in the mid-1990s for his research on the authenticity of the 1216 *Privilege of Poverty*. In brief, he argued that Innocent III's document, along with Clare's *Testament* (which is the only medieval document to refer to the earlier *Privilege* explicitly) were later medieval forgeries, produced in reformed Clarissan scriptoria in the late fifteenth century and circu-

---

[24] The inspiration for this organization presumably comes from Francis's *Later Rule* of 1223 (the *Regula Bullata*), which also was originally a continuous text. His rule was an important model for Clare's.

[25] There is a lengthy description of the manuscript (its physical characteristics, binding, handwriting, etc.) in Attilio Bartoli Langeli, *Gli autografi di frate Francesco e di frate Leone*. Corpus Christianorum Autographa Medii Aevi 5 (Turnhout: Brepols, 2000), 108-24. Plates XII-XXVII provide photographs of the manuscript.

[26] For example, Diego Ciccarelli, "Contributi alla recensione degli scritti di S. Chiara," *Miscellanea Francescana* 79 (1979): 347-74; Engelbert Grau, "Die Schriften der Heiligen Klara und die Werke ihrer Biographen," *Movimento Religioso Femminile e Francescanesimo nel secolo XIII. Atti del VII Convegno Internationale, Assisi, 11-13 ottobre, 1979* (Assisi: Società Internazionale di Studi Francescani, 1980), 195-238.

lated through likeminded communities by means of manuscripts such as the Messina codex. A recent study, however, has challenged his conclusions with important implications for the transmission of Clare's writings, including her rule.[27]

Attilio Bartoli Langeli examined the Messina manuscript as part of a broader study of the autograph manuscripts of Francis and his companion and secretary, Brother Leo. His paleographical and historical analysis concluded that Leo likely had produced the Messina manuscript during the decade between 1253-1263 as a way of preserving Clare's writings and her testimony to the early ideals of the Lesser Brothers.[28] As a frequent visitor to San Damiano in the years following Francis's death, Bartoli Langeli reasons that Leo may have taken on a similar secretarial role for Clare, assisting with her correspondence and perhaps the drafting of the rule.[29] The Messina codex appears to be a unique compilation of Clare's writing, but Leo's involvement (or even that of another friar-scribe) raises the question of how many copies of her rule existed in this critical decade. Or, more accurately, how

---

[27] See Werner Maleczek, "Das '*Privilegium Paupertatis*' Innocenz III. Und das Testament der Klara von Assisi. Überlegungen zur Frage ihrer Echtheit." *Collectanea Franciscana* 65 (1995): 5-82. ["Questions about the Authenticity of the Privilege of Poverty of Innocent III and of the Testament of Clare of Assisi," trans. Cyprien Rosen and Dawn Nothwehr, *Greyfriars Review* 12 (1998): 1-80.] The English translation follows the Italian translation of the article, which includes some revisions and Maleczek's responses to his critics. For the impact of the debate on studies of Clare and Franciscan women, see Lezlie Knox, "Clare of Assisi: Foundress of an Order?," *Spirit and Life* 11 (2004): 11-31. See the essay on Clare's *Testament* in this volume.

[28] Bartoli Langeli, *Gli autografi di frate Francesco*, 125-29. While scholars have been cautious about Leo's role as scribe (Bartoli Langeli himself notes that Leo's hand is not particularly distinct, 91), most concur with his dating of the manuscript to the middle of the thirteenth century. For the reception of Bartoli Angeli's arguments, see the comments of Enrico Menestò, "Lo stato attuale degli studi su Chiara d'Assisi," in *Clara claris praeclara: l'esperienza cristiana e la memoria di Chiara d'Assisi in occasione del 750. anniversario della morte: atti del Convegno internazionale: Assisi, 20-22 novembre 2003* (Assisi: Edizioni Porziuncola, 2004), 4-8. This very useful conference volume (hereafter cited as *Clara claris praeclara*) focuses on the current state of Clarian studies.

[29] For the relationship between Leo, Clare, and the San Damiano community, see Bartoli Langeli, *Gli autografi di frate Francesco*, 93-103. Alfonso Marini earlier had proposed such a role for Leo in "Gli Scritti di Santa Chiara e la Regola," *Chiara di Assisi: Atti del XX Convegno internazionale, Assisi, 15-17 ottobre 1992* (Spoleto: Centro Italiano di Studi sull'alto Medioevo, 1993), 128 note 58.

many versions were extant since there are notable structural differences between the Assisi and Messina manuscripts.

Unlike the Assisi parchment, which presents a continuous text of *The Rule of Saint Clare*, the Messina codex is divided into twelve chapters, marked by initial letters and rubricated headings.[30] It also includes both *Solet annuere* and Cardinal Rainaldo's *Quia vos*, but the order of the documents differs. The Assisi manuscript begins with the bulls of approbation, followed by the complete text of the rule in a continuous format, before closing with the final clauses of the papal bull and its date of approval. The Messina codex presents the rule first (ff. 1r-18v).[31] It concludes with the date of approval from the cardinal's bull and the final clauses of *Solet annuere* with its later date of approval (ff. 18v-19r). The manuscript next includes the *Privilege of Poverty* (ff. 19v-21r) and only then the opening of *Solet annuere* and the body of *Quia vos* (ff. 21r-22v). These differences could indicate that the papal chancery dropped the chapters during the hasty process of transcription or that a new version was presented for papal approval since chapters would make it appear more like a legislative document. The most compelling possibility, though, is that Leo was working from a different version of the rule than what had been presented to the papal chancery. Felice Accrocca has suggested that this putative source could be a version that had been approved by Cardinal Rainaldo, thus explaining the different order of the documents in Messina codex.[32]

The structural differences between the Assisi and Messina manuscripts raise questions about whether it is really appropriate to refer to

---

[30] Other chapter divisions of the rule also circulated during the Middle Ages, but were considerably less well known. A late medieval vernacular example (with fourteen chapters) has been published as *L'antico volgarizzamento della Regola di S. Chiara che con parecchie notizie viene in luce nel dì in cui dopo cinquant' anni ritorna al divin culto la chiesa già ad essa Santa in Verona dedicata* (Verona: Tipograia Civelli, 1860). The inventory of the library of Corpus Domini in Bologna lists a shortened version (perhaps a hybrid of several rules), albeit in thirteen chapters: "Le Regole di S. Chiara, redotte a brevità dalla Santa sede apostolica in 13 soli capitoli, scritte a penna et ligati in carta capretta." See Serena Spanò Martinelli, "La biblioteca del 'Corpus Domini' bolognese: l'inconsueto spaccato di una cultura monastica femminile," in *La Bibliofilía* 88 (1986), 17.

[31] See Bartoli Langeli, *Gli autografi di frate Francesco*, 112-14.

[32] Felice Accrocca, "L'Illiterato e il suo testimone: considerazioni sull'autografia di frate Francesco e frate Leone in margine ad un recente volume," *Collectanea Franciscana* 72 (2002): 337-55. [English translation: "The "Unlettered One" and His Witness: Footnotes to a Recent Volume on the Autographs of Brother Francis and Brother Leo," trans. Edward Hagman, *Greyfriars Review* 16 (2002): 265-82.]

the former document as the "original form" of *The Rule of Saint Clare*. Over a quarter century ago, Chiara Augusta Lainati, a Clarissan nun and scholar of Clare's life and writings, wrote that the Protomonastery has numerous copies of the rule dating from the mid-thirteenth century.[33] These manuscripts remained mostly unstudied, however, until 2001 when a research project undertaken by the Umbrian Clarissan Federation encouraged new codicological investigations.[34] These sisters already have corrected the readings of some words in the edition of the *Rule of Saint Clare* based on collating the text of the Assisi parchment with the original bulls of reconfirmation from 1266 and 1343.[35] Their project also has provided an opportunity for a rigorous reexamination of the Assisi manuscript, on par with that received by the Messina codex.

In May 2006 Stefano Brufani and Attilio Bartoli Langeli studied the Assisi manuscript and later had new photographs prepared of it.[36] Their detailed analysis, which takes into account both paleographical and historical evidence, convincingly demonstrates that the Assisi parchment is not Pope Innocent IV's 1253 confirmation, but rather Pope Clement IV's 1266 reissue of *Solet annuere*. Its identification as the original text comes from an annotation recorded during the later

[33] Chiara Augusta Lainati, "Le Fonti riguardanti il Secondo Ordine Francescano delle Sorelle Povere di Sancta Chiara," *Forma Sororum* 23 (1986): 141. Among her numerous publications, she is the author of the introduction to the *Rule of Saint Clare* in the Italian source collection *Fonti Francescane nuova edizione* (Padua: Editrici Francescane, 2004), 1753-58.

[34] The Federazione di S. Chiara di Assisi delle Clarisse di Umbria-Sardegna formed a research team of fourteen sisters, joined by the noted Franciscan scholar Felice Accrocca, with the goal of rediscovering Clare's evangelical teachings through a close study of her rule. They have published three volumes to date: an examination of the rule's legislative sources, a general study of Clare, and a commentary on the rule (cited in the bibliography and in subsequent notes; see also notes 18 and 21 above). For a preliminary summary of their findings; see Chiara Agnese Acquadro and Chiara Christiana Mondonico, "La Regola di Chiara di Assisi: Il Vangelo come forma di vita," in *Clara claris praeclara*, 147-48.

[35] The corrected readings include: Prologue *incluso/inclusae*; 2:8 *potuerit/poterit*; 4:18 *minori/iuniori*; 4:20 *recipant/recipiatur*; 5:17 *prudentia/providentia*; 7:1 *laboritio/laborerio*; 9:17 *prudentia/providentia*; and 12:11 *defunctorum/defunctarum*.

[36] Stefano Brufani and Attilio Bartoli Langeli, "La lettera Solet annuere di Innocenzo IV per Chiara d'Assisi (9 agosto 1253)," *Franciscana* 8 (2006): 63-106. They were accompanied by Giovanni Boccali and two Clarisses, Abbess Chiara Damiano Tiberio and Chiara Agnese Acquadro, a member of the research team. The resulting photographs accompany the article, see plates 7-12.

seventeenth or early eighteenth century (*"Originale della Regola di S. Chiara"*), perhaps added at the same time that the parchment was entombed with Clare. Brufani, whose half of the article focuses on the historical development of the memory of Clare and her rule, argues that the 1266 document was buried as a relic in the modern era to emphasize her relationship to Francis, whose *Later Rule* also was preserved as a relic in Assisi.[37] The recovery of this parchment during the second half of the nineteenth century led to what has been the common scholarly understanding that this copy of *Solet annuere* was Pope Innocent IV's original 1253 text.[38]

It is unclear what happened to the pope's copy. The bull approving Clare's *forma vitae* was not recorded in the papal register so when the sisters in Assisi sought its reconfirmation in 1266 to guarantee that they were not required to profess Pope Urban IV's new constitution, they may have sent the original copy to the papal court.[39] This may seem extraordinary to us since we are accustomed to think of the Assisi parchment as the original text with a precious connection to Clare. Perhaps the sisters were worried about its reconfirmation and so sent the original copy as added pressure.[40] It seems likely that there were multiple copies of Clare's *forma vitae* in the sisters' archive in Assisi in the middle of the thirteenth century. When they received the 1266 reconfirmation, it joined the others in the sisters' archive.[41] These copies are only beginning to receive scholarly attention. Comparison of their texts will provide further evidence about the transmission of the *Rule of Saint Clare*. Indeed, the Franciscan research team already has identified two "streams" of transmission for the text—an official one through the

---

[37] Brufani-Bartoli Langeli, "La lettera Solet annuere," 82 and 85-88. However, a manuscript conservator who subsequently examined the parchment judged that it seems to have been handled frequently as a common document, not a relic. See Federazione S. Chiara di Assisi, *Il Vangelo*, 22.

[38] Brufani-Bartoli Langeli, "La lettera Solet annuere," 90.

[39] Brufani-Bartoli Langeli, "La lettera Solet annuere," 100.

[40] For the sisters' commitment to Clare's *forma vitae*, see Felice Accrocca, "Chiara e l'Ordine Francescano," in *Clara Claris Praeclara*, 350-54.

[41] It is worth emphasizing that there were (at least) two copies of the 1266 reconfirmation in Assisi. There was the original papal bull, which was divided into chapters, and the Assisi parchment, which has the continuous text and was later buried as a relic in Clare's tomb. Presumably these were produced around the same time in the papal chancery. Whether the continuous text was meant to replace the 1253 original copy of *Solet annuere* is unknown.

papal chancery (the diplomatic) and an unofficial one (non-diplomatic) within the Order and especially its female communities.[42]

In sum, the Assisi parchment from the Protomonastery dates from 1266. Its famous notes refer to *Solet annuere*'s reconfirmation and its creation in the papal chancery in that year.[43] The handwriting is faded and very difficult to read (made more difficult by Cozza-Luzi's late nineteenth-century chemical treatments). Nonetheless, Attilio Bartoli Langeli was able to correct several readings. The initial "S," which had been identified as Innocent IV's mark, is actually a "G," a signature from the chancery scribe who wrote "ad instar fiat." This was a common diplomatic formula indicating that the bull was a reissue, with this copy intended to become the new exemplar.[44] The other note is in a different hand and indicates that a correction was made to the text.[45] The fourteenth-century note which seemed to confirm Clare's contact with the document actually refers more generically to the many who had kissed it out of their own devotion.[46] Brufani and Bartoli Langeli thus have shown that while we cannot directly connect the Assisi manuscript to Clare and the original approval of her *forma vitae*, it does provide important evidence that copies of the rule were available in Assisi for those who were interested in it.

The number of copies was limited, however, and the *Rule of Saint Clare* was mostly forgotten over the next century and a half. There is no evidence that Clare's *forma vitae* influenced other thirteenth-century Franciscan rules for women such as those composed by Isabelle of France or Pope Urban IV. Queen Sancia of Mallorca, who received

---

[42] See Federazione S. Chiara di Assisi, *Il Vangelo*, 39-40 for general comments. Brief descriptions of key manuscripts follow. The official diplomatic tradition appears in four texts (40-43): the 1266 Assisi manuscript, a 1343 copy obtained by Sancia of Mallorca, and two fifteenth-century French manuscripts associated with the reform movement begun by Colette of Corbie. Medieval scholars use the term diplomatics to refer to official documents, such as papal letters, charters, and notarial instruments.

[43] As with Maleczek's interest in the Messina Codex, the unusual situation of these notes attracted their attention. It is very rare for bulls from this period to have notes on them, see Brufani-Bartoli Langeli, "La lettera Solet annuere," 93.

[44] Brufani-Bartoli Langeli, "La lettera Solet annuere," 94-96. The name is abbreviated and seems to be a G followed by a lowercase a. Bartoli Langeli notes that it is unlikely to refer to Pope Clement IV, whose birth name was Guido (104).

[45] Brufani-Bartoli Langeli, "La lettera Solet annuere," 99-100 and 104-05. The word *filias* was omitted in the original copy and later added (see, FLCl 6:3).

[46] Brufani-Bartoli Langeli, "La lettera Solet annuere," 106. ... *tetigit et obsculata est pro devotione pluribus et pluribus vicibus.*

permission for the convents she founded in Naples to profess the *Rule of Saint Clare*, is an exceptional example of fourteenth-century interest in the rule.[47] Presumably the queen obtained a copy of the rule from Assisi since its 1343 reconfirmation survives in the Protomonastery's archive. Queen Sancia's interest in the *Rule of Saint Clare* may have grown out of her support for the Franciscans spirituals, who were interested in a return to its earlier ideals. Perhaps surprisingly given the Spiritual's commitment to the ideal of evangelical poverty, Sancia was not attracted to the rule for its stance on possessions – her foundations were very well endowed as Bruzelius has shown. Rather, these communities were double houses and Clare's *forma vitae* allowed for a mutually supportive relationship between the brothers and sisters. Sancia's reforms, however, were limited to Naples and seem to have had little influence over Franciscans communities elsewhere on the Italian peninsula.

The relationship between the constitutions composed by the French reformer Colette of Corbie and Clare's *forma vitae* deserves further study. Colette, who originally had professed the vows of the penitential order and lived as a recluse, was interested in returning the Franciscan Order to its original, stricter observance. In 1410 she obtained a copy of Clare's *forma vitae* from Assisi and used it as the basis for her statutes.[48] This text followed the earlier rule in insisting upon a strict interpretation of poverty, but it also expanded on other aspects, particularly in developing liturgical practices and devotional life within the community. By the time of Colette's death in 1447, eighteen convents in France (including both reformed and newly founded houses) followed her statutes.[49] The extent to which this text influenced other

[47] For a fascinating discussion of Sancia's religious patronage and identification with the early Franciscan movement, see Caroline Bruzelius, *The Stones of Naples: Church Building in Angevin Italy, 1266-1343* (New Haven: Yale University Press, 2005), 133-54.

[48] Originally Colette obtained the rule for her own community in Besançon, where the manuscript is still held; see Brufani-Bartoli Langeli, "La lettera Solet annuere," 81. For Colette's religious ideals and her modifications to the *Rule of Saint Clare*, a useful introduction is Élisabeth Lopez, "Sainte Colette," in *Sainte Claire d'Assise et sa posterité VIIIè centenaire de Sainte Claire. Actes du Colloque de l'UNESCO (29 septembre-1èr octobre 1994)*, ed. Geneviève Brunel-Lobichon, et al. (Paris: Les Éditions franciscaines, 1994), 203-09.

[49] Pope Benedict XIII had given Colette permission to reform or found new communities in 1406. The pope also commissioned friars to assist her. See BF VI, 347.

reformers is not clear. Pious tradition suggests Colette inspired Italian Clarisses such as Cecilia Coppoli and Paola Malatesta, as well as John of Capistrano, Vicar General for the Observance, but there seems to be limited evidence for interest in her statutes south of the Alps.[50] Instead, interest in returning to Clare's own *forma vitae* developed.

It was not until the 1440s that adoption of the *Rule of Saint Clare* became widespread thanks to its promotion by friars and sisters connected with the Regular Observance.[51] Manuscript copies of the *Rule of Saint Clare* in both Latin and vernacular versions circulated among the reformed houses, in many cases carried by the women who moved between houses to bring about the renewal. These are the manuscripts which the Franciscan research team refers to as the non-official (non-diplomatic) tradition.[52]

The convent of Santa Chiara in Urbino is a representative example of the social and spiritual networks that connected these reformed communities.[53] In central Italy, Monteluce in Perugia and Santa Lucia in Foligno were at the heart of the reform movement. In 1455 several sisters were sent from Monteluce to establish a new house in Urbino. Later other sisters from Santa Lucia joined them. One of these convents – both had active scriptoria – may have provided a copy of the *Rule of Saint Clare* for the new community.[54] A fifteenth-century manu-

---

[50] For these contacts, see Élisabeth Lopez, *Culture et Sainteté: Colette de Corbie (1381-1447)*, (St. Etienne: CERCOR, 1994) [English translation *Colette of Corbie (1381-1447) Learning and Holiness*, trans. Joanna Waller, ed. Elise Saggau (St. Bonaventure, NY: Franciscan Institute Publications, 2011).] I have raised questions about Colette's influence on John of Capistrano, see Lezlie S. Knox, *Creating Clare of Assisi: Female Franciscan Identities in Later Medieval Italy* (Leiden: Brill, 2008), 133-34. A partial explanation for Colette's limited influence may be that she refused to unite her reform movement with the Italian Observants.

[51] For Observant Reform within the Order of Saint Clare see Antonio Fantozzi, "La riforma osservante dei monasteri delle clarisse nell'Italia centrale. Documenti sec. XV-XVI," *Archivum Franciscanum Historicum* 23 (1930): 361-82 and 488-550; Alfonso Marini, "Il recupero della memoria di Chiara nell'osservanza," in *Clara Claris Praeclara*, 525-38; Mario Sensi, "L'Osservanza francescana al femminile," *Bailammé: Rivista di Spiritualità* 6 (1992): 139-61.

[52] Federazione di Santa Chiara, *Il Vangelo*, 43-64.

[53] See Fausta Casolini, "Origini del monastero federiciano di Santa Chiara in Urbino," *Chiara d'Assisi: Rassegna del Protomonastero* 5 (1957): 87-98.

[54] Monteluce's own convent chronicle, a product of this *scriptoria*, discusses the foundation of the community in Urbino "de l'Ordine et Regula de Sancta Chiara." See *Memoriale di Monteluce. Cronaca del monastero delle Clarisse di Perugia dal 1448 al 1838*,

script still preserved in the convent library in Urbino includes a Latin copy of Clare's *forma vitae* that appears to have been copied from a text closely related to the "original" Assisi document.[55] The Urbino manuscript also includes Pope Eugenius IV's bull calling for the universal reform of the Order of Saint Clare (*Ordinis tui*, from May 12, 1431),[56] and a commentary on the rule which the sisters at Corpus Christi in Mantua had commissioned from John of Capistrano, who was a strong supporter of the reformed women.[57] Corpus Christi became the center for female reform in northern Italy and helped spread both John of Capistrano's commentary and Clare's own writings.

The Urbino manuscript also contains a vernacular version of the *Rule of Saint Clare*, her *Testament*, and the *Benediction*. Another manuscript in the sisters' library contains only the vernacular texts.[58] It may have been common for reformed Clarissan houses to have copies of Clare's rule in both Latin and vernacular copies. Two manuscripts from Montevergine in Messina contain versions of the rule in the Sicilian vernacular.[59] These vernacular translations have not been studied systematically and deserve more attention for what they can reveal about the transmission of the *Rule of Saint Clare*.[60]

It is legitimate to ask to what degree Clare can be considered as author of the text, not in the least since she always gave authorial credit to Francis. The text famously opens with the claim that it is "the form of life of the Order of the Poor Sisters that blessed Francis instituted (FLCl 1:1-3)." It later incorporates the *forma vivendi* that Francis had

---

ed. Chiara Augusta Lainati (Santa Maria degli Angeli-Assisi: Edizioni Porziuncola, 1983), 17-18.

[55] Ciccarelli, "Contributi," 353-54; Federazione S. Chiara di Assisi, *Il Vangelo*, 56-58.

[56] *Bullarium Franciscanum*, New Series I, 16.

[57] See Donatus van Andrichem, "Explicatio Primae Regulae S. Clarae auctore S. Ioanne Capistratensis (1445)," *Archivum Franciscanum Historicum* 22 (1929): 337-57 and 512-29. For a discussion of his commentary, see Lezlie Knox, "'One and the Same Spirit' (2 Cel 204): The Friars and Sisters in Spiritual Union," *Franciscan Studies* 64 (2006): 235-54.

[58] Ciccarelli, "Contributi," 354-55.

[59] Diego Ciccarelli, "Volgarizzamenti siciliani inediti degli scritti di S. Chiara," *Schede Medievali* 4 (1983): 19-51.

[60] This project looks to become another outcome of the Franciscan research team's efforts. See Monica Benedetta Umiker, "Il Volgarizzamento della "il Regola di S. Chiara e le "Ordinazioni di Monteluce" secondo il ms. 25 della Chiesa Nuova in Assisi," *Archivum Franciscanum Historicum* 102 (2009): 175-225.

given to San Damiano (FLCl 6:6, 3-4), while other sections certainly adapted parts of the spiritual directions he gave to the sisters, even if they are not labeled as such.[61] Clare's *forma vitae* also included passages taken from the friars' *Later Rule* and followed its structure. For these reasons and even more fundamentally because she insisted that the sisters were living according to the spiritual ideals they shared with Francis, for Clare it was obvious that Francis should be recognized as the author of their form of life.

Later medieval chroniclers accepted this claim and understood it as the reason for the conformities between the *Rule of Saint Clare* and the friars' own text.[62] Ubertino of Casale,[63] the compiler of the *Chronica XXIV Generalium*,[64] Nicholas Glassberger,[65] and Mariano of Florence all identify Francis as its author.[66] The first printed edition of the rule, the *Firmamentum Trium Ordinum* published in Paris in 1512, also acknowledged Francis as its author, as did the famous seventeenth-century annalist, Luke Wadding. His *Annales Minorum* incorporated the rule in the events of 1224, presumably when Francis presented the

---

[61] Clare refers to his guidance in her third letter to Agnes of Prague where she explains both Francis's directives for fasting and how the sisters at San Damiano had practiced them (LAg 3, 29-41). Cardinal Rainaldo also cited this mix of directions in *Quia vos*: "… we ratify this form of life … that your Father Saint Francis gave to you for your guidance in word and mouth."

[62] See Livarius Oliger, "De origine regularum Ordinis S. Clarae," *Archivum Franciscanum Historicum* 5 (1912): 432-34.

[63] Ubertino da Casale, *Arbor vitae cruxifixae Jesu Christi*, vol. 6 (Turin: Bottega d'Erasmo, 1961). Ubertino does not seem to have known the text of Clare's rule, only that there was a different rule than the Urbanist one which most sisters then professed.

[64] *Analecta Franciscana* III, 274. This text was an important source for later chroniclers so it is useful to quote in full: *Anno Domini MCCLII, XVI kalendas Octobris, dominus Raynaldus, Cardinalis et episcopus Hostiensis, Ordinis Protector auctoritate papali, in Perusio Curia residente, regulam, quam beatus Franciscus sanctae Clarae et suis sororibus tradiderat observandam, regulae fratrum Minorum multum conformem, confirmavit et sigilli sui munimine roboravit, pontificatus domini Innocentii Papae IV anno X.*

[65] *Analecta Franciscana* II, 72. Glassberger wrote his *Chronica Ordinis Minorum Observantium* between 1506-1508. It provides a useful testimony to what represented "common knowledge" at the end of the Middle Ages.

[66] Mariano of Florence, *Libro delle degnità et excellentie del Ordine della seraphica madre delle povere donne Sancta Chiara da Asisi*, ed. Giovanni Boccali (Florence: Edizioni Studi Francescani, 1986), paragraph 57 especially, but there are numerous other examples. Mariano wrote the first history dedicated to the Order of Saint Clare between 1515-1519. He includes a lengthy analysis of the conformities between the brothers' and sisters' orders, in which their rules are one example.

text in its surviving form to the sisters at San Damiano.[67] Lest this list appear to confirm a "misogynist suppression" of Clare's authorial contribution, it should be noted that late medieval Clarisses also identified Francis as the author of this rule. For example, while Sister Battista Alfani's *Vita et Leggenda della Vergine Sancta Chiara* adds details about how Cardinal Rainaldo and Pope Innocent IV confirmed the rule, she always refers to it as the form of life Francis had given to the sisters.[68] The rediscovery, and indeed celebration, of Clare's authorial voice primarily resulted from the interest in recovering the voices of medieval women authors that gained momentum in the 1980s.[69] Most scholars today identify Clare as author of the rule, recognizing its inspiration in Francis's writings as well as her deliberate invocation of his authority.[70]

Scholars also stress the creative ways in which her voice appears in the rule. The best-known passages in the rule are the autobiographical references in the sixth chapter which recount the origins of San Damiano as well as the sisters' commitment to evangelical poverty (FLCl 6:1-2, 10-15), which are bracketed by Francis's *forma vivendi* and his *Testament* for the Sisters (FLCl 6:7-9).[71] Her original contributions ap-

---

[67] *Annales Minorum* II, 77-84.

[68] See Battista Afani, *Vita et Leggenda della Seraphica Vergine Sancta Chiara*, ed. Giovanni Boccali (Santa Maria degli Angeli-Assisi: Edizioni Porziuncola, 2004), examples on 245 and 258-59. Battista, a sister at Monteluce, based her vernacular legend on the Latin *Legend of Saint Clare*, but typically added more details and descriptions drawn from other chronicles (e.g. Bartolomeo of Pisa's *Conformities*) as well as Clare's canonization process, which seems to be the source for these events (Monteluce had a vernacular copy of the PC). For further discussion of Battista's scribal activities and her legend, see Lezlie Knox, "What Francis Intended: Gender and the Transmission of Knowledge in the Franciscan Order," in *Seeing and Knowing: Women and Learning in Medieval Europe, 1200-1500*, ed. Anneke Mulder-Bakker (Turnhout: Brepols, 2004), 143-61.

[69] For the growth of the study of medieval women, see the comments in Paul Freedman and Gabrielle Spiegel, "Medievalisms Old and New: The Rediscovery of Alterity in North American Studies," *American Historical Review* 103 (1998): 677-704. Interest in Clare developed somewhat later than other medieval religious women. She was not included, for example, in Peter Dronke's seminal *Women Writers of the Middle Ages: A Critical Studies of Texts from Perpetua (d. 203) to Marguerite Porete (d. 1310)* (Cambridge: Cambridge University Press, 1984).

[70] A recent calculation grants 63.12% of the text to Clare, see Federazione S. Chiara di Assisi, *Il Vangelo*, 75.

[71] Given the importance of this chapter, it is surprising that the excerpts chosen for a collection of medieval monastic rules skip these and other passages that speak to

pear most clearly in the sections on life within the community. Here Clare offers a democratic ideal of religious life where decisions are reached through consultation, and thus presents the abbess as the servant of the other sisters (see FLCl 4:8-17, 8:12-21, 10:1-7).

Other passages indicate the efforts of a team of collaborators to work with Clare so as to both incorporate her Franciscan ideals, and ensure that the text would meet canonical standards. Regrettably we do not know how this team functioned. No medieval descriptions of working on the rule have survived that might enlighten the circumstances of its composition and subsequent transmission. Several of the sisters told the papal investigators that Clare spun thread and embroidered altar cloths while she was ill in bed toward the end of her life, but they say nothing about the composition of her *forma vitae* taking place during those years.[72] Indeed, these women were surely among her most important collaborators, although they do not often receive credit.[73] A hint of their discussions (or at least the circumstances for them) appears in the rule. It calls for a weekly chapter meeting at which the abbess should "consult with all her sisters concerning whatever concerns the welfare and good of the monastery, for the Lord frequently reveals what is better to the youngest."[74]

There is much speculation about the identity of her other collaborators. Brother Leo's participation seems to have been more than merely scribal. Felice Accrocca has suggested that Leo or another

---

the distinctive Franciscan character of life at San Damiano. Instead, the editors chose sections of the rule that are more traditionally monastic (chapters 1, 2, 5 and 11). The introduction to the text also fails to make clear the limited audience for the rule and suggests it governed all the "Poor Clares." See *Regular Life: Monastic, Canonical and Mendicants Rules*, ed. Douglas McMillan and Kathryn Smith Fladenmuller (Kalamazoo: TEAMS, 1997), 75-80.

[72] See PC 1:6 and 6:14.

[73] Felice Accrocca is one of the few scholars to discuss the contributions of Clare's sisters (perhaps drawing upon his experiences working with the Clarissan research team). See his comments in Chiara d'Assisi, *Le Regola, le Lettere, e il Testamento Spirituale: tutti gli scritti della santa di Assisi* (Monferrato: Piemme, 2004), 29.

[74] This description of the chapter is Clare's original contribution. It also is one of the passages where the reading was corrected by the Clarissan research team. Previously scholars had read "minori" – consult with the least [of the sisters] – as a reference to Franciscan *minoritas* (but with parallels to the *Rule of Saint Benedict*). However, reexamination of the Assisi manuscript corrected this word to *iuniori* (youngest). See Chiara Agnese Acquadrato, "*Saepe enim Dominus quod melius est minori revelat.* Un errore di lettura ormai vecchio cinque secoli," *Collectanea Franciscana* 71 (2001): 521-26.

member of the circle of friars who were closest to Francis may have helped to incorporate sections of the friars' *Later Rule*.[75] After the Poverello's death, these men understandably gravitated to San Damiano, where Clare and her sisters had lived for over a decade. These brothers – Elias, Angelo, Juniper, Ruffino, Philip Longo, and Leo – could have worked with Clare to make clear how the women were also living out Francis's ideals against the efforts of the Papal curia to regularize them.[76] They also may have been able to help put the rule into a more juridical form, but it seems more likely that a cleric associated with the papal court may have helped.[77] Cardinal Rainaldo de' Segni, who had served as the sisters' protector since 1228, has been identified as a likely candidate. While he was not especially sympathetic to the sisters' desire to live without material support, the *Legend of Saint Clare* acknowledges that Clare sought his efforts to secure a reconfirmation of San Damiano's *Privilege of Poverty*.[78] He visited San Damiano in November 1251 at which time Clare seems to have sought his intervention. Presumably up until his confirmation of the rule the following September, he negotiated with Clare over the juridical requirements of the rule. His influence (or that of another clerical advisor) is most evident in the sections of the rule which draw from earlier monastic

---

[75] Accrocca, "L'Illiterato e il suo testimone," 352-53. Maria Pia Alberzoni also addresses this theme in "Chiara d'Assisi e il Vangelo come forma di vita," *Franciscana* 10 (2008): 223-54.

[76] On Clare's relationship with these friars and their possible contributions to the rule, see Maria Pia Alberzoni, "Chiara e San Damiano tra Ordine minoritico e curia papale," in *Clara claris praeclara*, 64-68.

[77] Chiara Agnese Acquadro and Chiara Christiana Mondonico identify the recently elected Franciscan Minister General John of Parma (1247-1257) as a possible source, but they do not indicate why. He would have the skills, but his motivation seems unlikely, even to the extent he admired Clare as one of Francis's earliest followers. See their article "La Regola di Chiara di Assisi: Il Vangelo come forma di vita," in *Clara Claris Praeclara*, 153. For the distancing of the Lesser Brothers from the enclosed women attached to the Order, see Lezlie Knox, "Audacious Nuns: Conflict between the Franciscan Friars and the Order of Saint Clare," *Church History* 41 (2000): 41-62.

[78] LCl 26. The sources have little to say about the cardinal's relationship with Clare during the 1240s so while scholars also assume she asked him to intervene on behalf of her rule, we have to be careful in describing his motives; see the comments of Alberzoni, "Clare and the Papacy," 57-61 (although she appears more open to his involvement in the recent "Chiara d'Assisi e il Vangelo come forma di vita").

legislation and that represent the canonical norms needed to secure the rule's approval.[79]

The somewhat awkward insertions of these passages have compelled some scholars to defend the originality of the *Rule of Saint Clare*.[80] However, as with her use of Francis's writings, close readings of the rule confirm that Clare's authorial voice emerges in her adaptations to Francis's rule for the friars and the papal constitutions to reflect her spiritual ideals and the needs of a community of religious women.

The *Rule of Saint Clare* crosses genres. In its structure and canonical status, it is a legislative text, specifically a constitution regulating a religious community. Such documents are usually identified as a *regula* or any of the related terms such as *statuta, instituta*, or *praecepta*.[81] But Clare never used any of those terms and always referred to it as the sisters' *forma vitae*, a phrase that appears seventeen times throughout the text, as well as four times in the *Testament*.[82] This phrase indicates how Clare conceived of the text less in a formal juridical way, and more as a source of spiritual direction. Jean-François Godet-Calogeras has observed that in its original form, that is, without the division into chapters, Clare's *forma vitae* looks more like a spiritual meditation than a legislative document.[83] This insight is important for understanding the interpretation of the text.

---

[79] Chapter four begins with an invocation of canonical norms for the election of the abbess. It is worth adding that this office itself is a reflection of these juridical requirements. Clare's legends recount how she had to be persuaded to accept the title of abbess, a hierarchal category which made her uncomfortable (see LCl 12).

[80] For example Margaret Carney, *The First Franciscan Woman: Clare of Assisi and Her Form of Life* (Quincy, IL: Franciscan Press, 1993), 81.

[81] For a discussion of the genre of monastic constitutions, see Gert Melville, "Regeln-*Consuetudines*-Texte-Statuten: Positionen für eine Typologie des normativen Schrifttums religiöser Gemeinschaften im Mittelalter," in *Regulae-Consuetudines-Statuta. Studi sulle fonti normative degli oridini religiosi nei secoli centrali del Medioevo*. Atti del I e del II Seminario internazionale di studio del Centro italo-tedesco di storia comparata degli ordini religiosi, ed. Cristina Andenna and Gert Melville (Münster: LIT, 2005), 5-25; Adalbert de Vogüé, *Les règles monastiques anciennes (400-700)*, Typologie des Sources du Moyen Âge Occidental 46 (Turnhout: Brepols, 1985).

[82] *Claire d'Assise: Écrits*, 41.

[83] Jean François Godet-Calogeras, "Structure of the *Form of Life* of Clare," *Spirit and Life* 11 (2004): 1-10. For rules as a form of religious instruction, see also Bert Roest, *Franciscan Literature of Religious Instruction before the Council of Trent* (Leiden:

II. Approaching the Text

While Francis's *forma vivendi* for the sisters and his *Later Rule* provided the starting point for Clare's rule, she and her collaborators also
made extensive use of other sources. Among the legislative sources, the
constitution for the Order of San Damiano, first composed by Cardinal Hugolino dei Segni in 1219, appears most frequently.[84] Some use
is made of the *Rule of Saint Benedict*,[85] Pope Innocent IV's rule, and
three other Franciscan rules: the constitution *"Praenarbonenses,"* Francis's *Earlier Rule*, and his *Rule for Hermitages*. In addition to these prescriptive texts, Clare's *forma vitae* also drew upon other early writings:
Francis's *Testament*, his *Letter to the Faithful*, and Thomas of Celano's
Remembrance of the Desire of a Soul. All editions of the *Rule of Saint
Clare* and most translations make clear where these borrowings occur,
either through different type fonts or other critical apparatus.[86] These
tools allow scholars to distinguish Clare's own voice from the passages
drawn from earlier sources.

Brill, 2004), 120-205. His discussion of Clare's *forma vitae*, however, is primarily a
description of its structure, 174-75.

[84] In addition to Oliger's foundational study ("De origine regularum"), other articles have studied the legal context of her rule. See Andrea Boni, "La legislazione
clariana nel contesto giuridico delle sue origini e della sua evoluzione," *Antonianum*
70 (1995): 47-98; Micheline de Fontette, *Les Religieuses à l'âge classique du droit canon:
recherches sur les structures juridiques des branches féminines des ordres* (Paris: J. Vrin, 1967),
128-51.

[85] The *Rule of Saint Benedict* was primarily a source of monastic tradition (e.g.,
the discussion of penance in FLCl 9: 1-9), compared to the Franciscan rules which
contribute actual language. For the Benedictine rule, see Henri de Sainte-Marie,
"Présence de la Règle Bénédictine dans la Règle de Sainte Claire," *Archivum Franciscanum Historicum* 82 (1989): 3-20 [English translation "Presence of the Benedictine
Rule in the Rule of St. Clare," *Greyfriars Review* 6 (1992): 49-65]. The inspiration for
Oliger's pioneering study of the *Rule of Saint Clare* in 1912 was to prove that it was not
a Benedictine constitution but rather one that drew on Franciscan traditions. See "De
Origine regularum," 182-85.

[86] For example, the *Sources Chrétiennes* edition uses regular capitals to indicate
borrowings from Francis's *Regula Bullata* and italicized capitals for other legislative
sources. Regis Armstrong's English translation (in common with the other editions)
includes extensive notes identifying both sources and similar passages that can be
found in Clare's other writings.

There is a long tradition of analyzing how the *Rule of Saint Clare* relates to these other texts, especially Francis's *Later Rule*.[87] A close comparison of the two documents makes clear that Clare wanted to incorporate as much of Francis's rule as was appropriate for a community of women. Chapters six and ten appear in their entirety, while parts of all the other chapters are included except for the ninth, which concerns the brothers who were preachers. Obviously, this is a topic that did not directly concern the women since they did not preach in public. Although Clare's *forma vitae* was divided into chapters to emphasize its relationship to Francis's *Later Rule*, the correspondence between the two is not precise. This division resulted in outwardly arbitrary groupings of chapters. For example, Clare's chapter nine discusses penance (chapter seven in the *Later Rule*), as well as the role of the serving sisters, those women who went outside San Damiano's walls to beg for alms in the community (a topic covered in chapter six of the *Later Rule*). While the flow is sometimes awkward (less obviously so without the chapter divisions), it nonetheless confirms that Clare felt free to adapt her sources.

A recent publication by the research team of Italian Clarisses has added to our understanding of how to read her rule in its juridical and spiritual contexts.[88] They produced a grid and system of fonts (both typefaces and colors) which show not only where Clare's *forma vitae* borrows from other rules, but also how the sisters' rule may be responding to them. This juxtaposition provides clear evidence of how often she adapted, and usually liberalized, her sources.[89] For example, her chapter five incorporates the decree from the Hugolinian Consti-

---

[87] The foundational study of their relationship is Engelbert Grau, "Die Regel der hl. Klara (1253) in ihrer Abhängigkeit von der Regel der Mindenbrüder," *Franziskanische Studien* 35 (1953): 211-71.

[88] Federazione delle Clarisse S. Chiara d'Assisi di Umbria-Sardegna, *Chiara di Assisi e le sue fonti legislative: Sinossi cromatica* (Padua: Edizioni Messaggero, 2003). Hereafter cited as Federazione, *Sinossi cromatica*.

[89] The grid has Clare's rule on the far left with its main sources following chronologically: The Rule of Saint Benedict, Hugolino's Constitution, Francis's Earlier Rule, the Later Rule, and Pope Innocent's Rule for the Order of San Damiano. One of the other benefits of the grid is that the notes offer further comparisons with other contemporary rules, for example the Dominican constitution of Montargis (for the enclosed sisters), the *Memoriale Praepositi* (for laity connected with the Dominican Order) and the rule for the Trinitarian Order. See the full list of sources in Federazione, *Sinossi cromatica*, 17-19.

tution which called for almost perpetual silence, but allows for some flexibility to be determined by the abbess. Reflecting this difference of attitude, Clare changed Cardinal Hugolino's *legem loquendi* to *formam loquendi* (FLCl 5:8), indicating a subtle shift away from the prescriptive quality of the papal rule.[90] With enclosure, she also modified the earlier strictures of the Hugolinian constitution with the statement that the abbess and her advisors could modify that requirement if necessary (FLCl 11:8). Where it was prudent to leave the canonical language intact, as in the requirements for the election of the abbess, Clare drew on Thomas of Celano's *Remembrance* to add details which presented a more pastoral image of that office.[91] This comparative method thus shows the real impact of monastic norms on Clare's *forma vitae*, but also her creativity and originality in defining how women could follow a Franciscan way of life.[92]

The first half of the thirteenth century was a critical period for both the growth in number of female followers of Francis as well as their legal status. Not surprisingly, Clare's saintly charisma has dominated the traditional understanding of that development following the claims of late medieval chronicles which describe the female Order as descended from the community at San Damiano. Fra Mariano of Florence's chronicle of the Order of Saint Clare, for example, explained how Francis had sent women from Assisi to found new houses which would follow the form of life he had given to Clare for San Damiano. So many women had been inspired by her to enter the order, Mariano added, that its numbers and fame spread rapidly through all of Italy with the aid of the Friars Minor.[93] Recent scholarship has challenged this traditional view. Historians have shown that Clare's direct influence was limited to a small network of houses with close ties to the San Damiano community. What became the Franciscan "Second Or-

---

[90] Compare FLHug 6.

[91] Compare 2C 185 and FLCl 4:10.

[92] These norms become apparent when comparing Clare's *forma vitae* with the papal legislation for both the Damianites and the female Dominican Order. See the discussion in Maria Pia Alberzoni, "Curia Romana e regolamentazione delle Damianite e delle Domenicane," in *Regulae—Consuetudines—Statuta. Studi sulle fonti normative degli oridini religiosi nei secoli centrali del Medioevo.* Atti del I e del II Seminario internazionale di studio del Centro italo-tedesco di storia comparata degli ordini religiosi, ed. Cristina Andenna and Gert Melville (Münster: LIT, 2005), 501-37.

[93] Mariano, *Libro delle degnità*, paragraph 51.

der" instead grew out of papal efforts to institutionalize the women's penitential movement in central Italy following monastic paradigms.[94] But even if Clare is no longer recognized as foundress of the female Franciscan Order, this research also has raised important new questions concerning the extent to which she sought to promote a competing model in challenge to the papal program. For if her *forma vitae* is not properly the culmination of the sisters' legislation as tradition has maintained,[95] its author did play a significant part in the complex and prolonged negotiations over the place of women in the medieval Franciscan Order. Indeed, Clare's rule is the product of lengthy debates over what represented the authentic form of female Franciscanism.

The early community at San Damiano was essentially a double order. As Clare tells us in her *forma vitae* and *Testament*, shortly after her religious conversion in 1212, she and a small group of women settled at San Damiano, where they lived according to the *forma vivendi* given to them by Francis. A small group of friars lived adjacent to the sisters' house in order to minister to them. Their mutual embrace of evangelical poverty bound the groups together and Clare's sisters thus were very much a part of the Early Brotherhood. Perhaps as early as 1216, she sent sisters to help establish similar foundations in Foligno, Perugia, Florence, and a few other places, but her efforts seem to have been limited primarily to towns near to Assisi. At the same time other female communities were forming independently, some of whom also had rejected the established religious orders in order to adopt a communal life based in radical poverty. The women's penitential movement was particularly dynamic in northern and central Italy, and historians have accordingly learned not to assimilate the diverse religious experiences

---

[94] The best introduction to this scholarship comes from the work of Maria Pia Alberzoni, who expands on earlier research by Clara Gennaro, Roberto Rusconi, and Lili Zarncke, among others. Several of her articles recently have been collected and translated into English as *Clare of Assisi and the Poor Sisters* (see footnote 22 and the bibliography). Although not yet translated, her lengthy study of the order's institutional development is equally important *La Nascita di un'Istituzione: L'Ordine di S. Damiano nel XIII secolo* (Milan: Edizioni CUSL, 1996).

[95] Compare Armstrong's comments that suggest a linear progression of a network of monasteries centered around Clare (*The Lady*, 33 and 89). The Urbanist rule, which more accurately represents the development of the sisters' legislation, usually is not included in the document collections since they focus almost exclusively on Clare's lifetime and canonization.

of these women to under one umbrella.[96] These groups were brought together primarily through the efforts of one man: Cardinal Hugolino de' Segni, the future Pope Gregory IX.

The cardinal first encountered penitential women when he was serving as cardinal legate in Tuscany and Lombardy. With Pope Honorius III's approval, Cardinal Hugolino began to regularize their communities around 1218. The earliest version of his monastic constitution for what he called the "Religion of the Poor Ladies of the Valley of Spoleto or of Tuscany (*religio pauperum dominarum de Valle Spoleti sive Tuscia*)" dates from the following year.[97] His rule imposed strict enclosure on the women, but it also granted them immunity from their local bishops so that their houses were directly dependent on Rome. Hugolino thus created the first religious order to consist solely of women.[98] For practical reasons, he was interested in associating them with an established order, preferably with the Order of Lesser Brothers who in some cases had helped found individual communities. Francis's strong opposition to strengthening ties between the brothers and female houses meant that the Cardinal was unable to appoint the

---

[96] For an introduction to this movement, see Herbert Grundmann, *Religious Movements in the Middle Ages: The Historical Links between Heresy, the Mendicant Orders, and the Women's Religious Movement in the Twelfth and Thirteenth Centuries*, 2nd revised edition, trans. Stephen Rowan (Notre Dame: University of Notre Dame Press, 1995). See also Jacques Dalarun, "Claire d'Assise et le mouvement féminin contemporain," in *Clara Claris Praeclara*, 381-402; Luigi Pellegrini, "Female Religious Experience and Society in Thirteenth-Century Italy," in *Monks and Nuns, Saints and Outcasts: Religion in Medieval Society. Essays in Honor of Lester K. Little*, ed. Sharon Farmer and Barbara Rosenwein (Ithaca, NY: Cornell University Press, 2000), 97-122.

[97] Simon Tugwell, "The Original Text of the *Regula Hugolini* (1219)," *Archivum Franciscanum Historicum* 93 (2000): 511-13. Ignacio Omaechevaria's collection of documents prints the 1228 revision, which previously had been thought to be the earliest surviving version of his constitution [see *Escritos de Santa Clara y Documentos Complementarios*. 3rd revised edition (Madrid: Biblioteca de Autores Cristianos, 1982), 217-32]. Hugolino's Constitution mandated that the sisters would profess the Benedictine Rule, following the Fourth Lateran Council's prohibition against new religious orders (see canon 13). This ban, enacted in 1215, meant that groups seeking recognition had to adopt one of the existing canonical rules.

[98] Examples of his regulations can be seen in the opening pages of the *Bullarium Franciscanum*, including the very first bull from August 27, 1218, see *Bullarium Franciscanum* I, 1-2. The earliest communities of the Cardinal's order were Monticelli located near Florence (BF I, 3-5), Lucca (BF I, 10-11), Siena (BF I, 11-13), and Monteluce in Perugia (BF I, 13-15). The inclusion of these documents in the *Bullarium* also represents a precocious identification of the Second Order.

Lesser Brothers to minister to them while Francis was alive. The situation changed, however, when Francis died in 1226 and Hugolino was elected pope the following year. In December 1227 Hugolino, now Pope Gregory IX, directed the Minister General to appoint brothers to the communities of Poor Ladies.[99]

Up to this point, San Damiano was not a part of the Hugolinian confederation. It had continued to serve as a home not only for the sisters, but also as a resting place for the brothers when they were in Assisi (including Francis, of course!).[100] The two groups were so linked by their spiritual ideals that no formal document had been thought necessary to confirm their bond. The Pope, however, now sought to bring Clare's house into his order. He had several reasons for doing so. On the one hand, San Damiano's connection with the friars buttressed their new responsibility to minister to the female order. But joining the Hugolinian confederation also would provide a regular constitution for Clare and her followers, bringing them closer to monastic norms. Indeed, Gregory seems to have hoped to make Clare's house the "model" for this new order. In 1228 he issued a revised constitution for what he now started to call the "Order of San Damiano (*Ordo Sancti Damiani*)." That same year, a letter introducing Cardinal Rainaldo de' Segni as the new protector for the twenty-four "poor monasteries of San Damiano of Assisi" lists Clare's house first even though she wanted little to do with the pope's program of increasing monasticization.[101] As Maria Pia Alberzoni has commented, "we are confronted with the paradox of an Order that takes the name of a monastery, which, however, does not consider itself a part of the Order."[102]

---

[99] *Bullarium Franciscanum* I, 36.

[100] Several of the sisters' told the papal investigators about a vision Clare had of Francis while he was recuperating at San Damiano, although its details (she nursed from his breast) made them uncomfortable and the scene was left out of her legends (compare PC 3:29, 4:51, 6:37, and 721). Elsewhere, they reported that Clare cured a brother who suffered from insanity (PC 2:15).

[101] This letter is printed in Omaechevaria, *Escritos de Santa Clara*, 356-61. An English translation appears in the second edition of Armstrong's Clare documents but it is omitted in the new edition. See Armstrong, *Clare of Assisi: Early Documents*, 2nd edition (St. Bonaventure, NY: Franciscan Institute Publications, 1993), 105-06.

[102] Alberzoni, "San Damiano in 1228," in *Clare of Assisi and the Poor Sisters*, 100.

Although she had agreed to accept the Hugolinian constitutions,[103] Clare resisted curial efforts to modify her house's unique character. This included not only their commitment to radical poverty, but also their close relationship with the Lesser Brothers. In 1228 she obtained the *Privilege of Poverty* guaranteeing that San Damiano could live without an endowment. This exception contradicted the requirement in the Hugolinian constitution that the women have support, although it is perhaps not as absolute a concession as the name may suggest. While Clare had sought complete poverty, the privilege stated only that the women could not be *compelled* to accept possessions. Gregory obviously hoped to persuade them to do so.[104] Two years later when the bull *Quo elongati* confirmed that the brothers could not enter female communities without papal permission, Clare reacted furiously to what she saw as an attack on San Damiano's attachment to the brothers.[105] She sent away the friars assigned to them, and threatened a hunger strike, protesting that if the sisters were to be deprived of the spiritual nourishment provided by the brothers' preaching, then they might as well give up ordinary food, too.[106] The pope reversed his ruling and confirmed that the Franciscan Minister General could appoint brothers to minister to the women's communities. These two confrontations marked a turning point in Clare's relationship with the papacy. Whereas she and Gregory had formerly had a warm friendship, friction now characterized their interactions.[107]

---

[103] For this reason, you sometimes will see references to Clare as a Benedictine or more commonly as having lived under the Benedictine Rule for over two decades [compare Ilia Delio, "Identity and Contemplation in Clare of Assisi's Writings," *Studies in Spirituality* 14 (2004): 139].

[104] The text appears in Armstrong, *The Lady*, 86-88. See also Mueller, *The Privilege of Poverty*, 39-41.

[105] The critical edition of *Quo elongati* is Herbert Grundmann, "Die Bulla 'Quo elongati' Papst Gregors IX," *Archivum Franciscanum Historicum* 54 (1961): 1-25 (the article includes commentary on the bull). An English translation of the text is printed in FA:ED 1, 570-75 (the relevant passage is on 575).

[106] See LCl 37.

[107] The earlier friendship is evident in a letter written by Gregory to Clare after he spent Holy Week at San Damiano in 1220; see the translation in Armstrong, *The Lady*, 129-30. This is the only letter that survived, although their correspondence is referred to in the *Legend of Saint Clare* (LCl 27).

Clare's major ally in protecting San Damiano's form of life now was Brother Elias.[108] He provided an important link to the Early Brotherhood and its spiritual ideals as the Lesser Brothers were becoming increasingly clericalized.[109] After his election as General Minister in 1232, Brother Elias became a strong advocate for Clare and San Damiano. There are brief but intriguing references in the sources that suggest Elias was helping to spread their form of life to other houses in opposition to the model of Hugolinian monasticism. Clare's sister Agnes, who had left San Damiano to live in the community at Monticelli outside Florence, wrote to her sister asking that she send Elias to visit them more often.[110] Perhaps with his assistance, Monticelli was able to obtain its own privilege of poverty, as did Monteluce (although their grant was rescinded two years later).[111]

The best evidence for Elias's activities on behalf of the sisters comes from Clare's letters to Agnes of Prague. She responded enthusiastically to the royal princess' desire to found a community modeled after San Damiano's way of life. Saint Francis in Prague similarly would be a double house and have no endowments so that they could

---

[108] Elias had visited San Damiano several times with Francis – in fact, he was the one who had persuaded Francis to visit the sisters on the occasion when he delivered the famous "Ashes" sermon (see 2C 207). For a reevaluation of Elias (whom the sources have frequently slandered), see Giulia Barone, *Da Frate Elia agli Spirituali* (Milan: Biblioteca Francescana, 1999). Alberzoni has identified his particular importance for Clare, see "Clare and the Papacy," 48-55; see also Michael Cusato, "Elias and Clare: An Enigmatic Relationship," in *Clare of Assisi: Investigations* (St. Bonaventure, NY: Franciscan Institute Publications, 1993), 95-115.

[109] This clericalization was related to *Quo elongati*'s attempt to reduce the brothers' access to female houses. Gregory was concerned that the brothers remain above reproach in their relations with the enclosed women, especially given their increased service to the ecclesiastical hierarchy.

[110] This is the only surviving letter between the two sisters (dating from 1229 or 1230), although most scholars assume there were others. It was included in the fourteenth-century *Chronica XXIV Generalium*, as a part of a *vita* of Agnes of Assisi; see the English translation in Armstrong, *The Lady*, 404-05. It is worth mentioning here that pious tradition claims Agnes also helped establish communities in Milan, Verona, and other cities but no contemporary evidence supports what was probably a later embellishment.

[111] *Bullarium Franciscanum* I, 50 and 73. Agnes of Assisi's above cited letter reported Monticelli's success immediately before referring to Elias.

rely solely on alms gathered by the resident brothers.[112] Clare may have sent Elias or other brothers to give support. Her second letter, dated between 1234-1238, recommended specifically that Agnes value Elias's counsel and disregard anyone who would try to direct the community against their vocation of evangelical poverty.[113] By "anyone" Clare surely meant Pope Gregory IX. He wanted all female houses to have endowments, a state that supported their identity as enclosed contemplatives. The pope also soon began to represent Francis as the founder of three orders – the Lesser Brothers, the cloistered Sisters, and the Penitents – a strategy that claimed Francis's saintly authority on behalf of his own (enclosed) Damianite Order.[114] At least part of his motivation was to respond to Clare and Elias, who had become the pope's primary adversaries in the development of legislative norms for female communities.[115]

Given their conflict, it is not too surprising that in 1238 when Agnes sought permission for her community in Prague to adopt the *forma vivendi* Francis had given to Clare and her sisters, Gregory denied her request. In his bull, *Angelis gaudium*, he contemptuously compared Francis's rule to infant formula, while his own Hugolinian constitution represented adult food.[116] He misleadingly claimed that the sisters at San Damiano no longer professed Francis's form of life, but rather now had adopted his own constitution. They had recognized the need for unity within the female order. If she believed otherwise, she had been misled by poor counsel (surely a veiled reference to Elias). Gregory concluded with the demand that Agnes recognize his authority as pope and do likewise. She did not. Joan Mueller's sensitive reading of Clare's third letter (also from 1238) shows how Clare encouraged Agnes both spiritually and pragmatically so that the younger woman was bolstered to continue her battle with the pope.[117] Agnes ultimately won

---

[112] For Saint Francis's planned status as a double house, see Christian-Frederik Feldskrau "*Hoc est quod cupio*: Approaching the Religious Goals of Clare of Assisi, Agnes of Bohemia, and Isabelle of France," *Magistra* 12 (2006): 21.

[113] 2 LAg 15-17.

[114] *Bullarium Franciscanum* I, 241-42; English translation in Armstrong, *The Lady*, 359-60.

[115] See Alberzoni, "Clare and the Papacy," 54. For the interactions between Clare, Agnes, and Gregory, also see Joan Mueller, *The Privilege of Poverty*, 53-88 esp.

[116] *Bullarium Franciscanum* I, 242-45; English translation in Armstrong, *The Lady*, 360-62.

[117] Mueller, *The Privilege of Poverty*, 82-85.

her own exemption for radical poverty, albeit in exchange for a greatly needed alliance with her brother, King Wenceslaus, as hostility grew between the pope and Emperor Frederick II.[118] Most religious women, of course, lacked Agnes of Prague's political connections and would not have been able to win similar concessions, even if they had wanted them. For as much as Pope Gregory viewed Clare (supported by Elias and now the well connected Agnes of Prague) as an antagonist in shaping juridical norms for female communities, it is unclear that the same interest in radical poverty was widespread among the variety of groups that the pope had united under the Damianite confederation.

Throughout the 1230s, Gregory eased the standard of poverty in many Damianite houses. He secured endowments for them and also limited the size of individual communities or moderated their fasting practices. Mueller characterized his actions as an attempt to undermine the sisters' vocational identity by reducing poverty to "pious flourishes."[119] Obviously his actions appear most acute in his dealings with Clare and Agnes, but in many of these cases the sisters seem to have been genuinely suffering for lack of alms. Few complaints survive about these changes.[120] This silence recalls the diversity within the Order of San Damiano: many communities had evolved outside inspiration from Francis and were motivated more by the eremetical life than by gospel poverty. Indeed, Clare herself was less interested in challenging the institutional character of the papal order than in seeking recognition of her alternative model derived from Francis through

---

[118] Mueller analyzes Agnes's political savvy, a topic missing in much of the English-language literature on Agnes; see Mueller, *The Privilege of Poverty*, 85-103 and 125-28. Agnes never won permission to follow Francis's *forma vivendi*. According to her hagiographical legend, her community was granted Clare's *forma vitae* sometime after 1253, but no surviving papal document confirms this permission. See Alfonso Marini, *Agnese di Boemia* (Rome: Istituto Storico dei Cappuccini, 1991), 90 note 20.

[119] Mueller, *The Privilege of Poverty*, 48. Also compare her comments on 52 and 66. In some cases she is clearly talking about Clare's or Agnes's interactions with the pope, but Mueller seems to see a more organized poverty movement with Clare as its leader than other scholars now credit.

[120] See Mueller, *The Privilege of Poverty*, 46-50 for examples of Gregory's relaxations. Siena is an exception where the women seem to have been unhappy with a proposed endowment. The pope worked out an arrangement similar to what the brothers had gained in *Quo elongati*. The sisters would not possess any temporal endowment, although they would have the use of the resulting funds (see *Bullarium Franciscanum* I, 116-17).

exemptions for San Damiano and other communities that shared her vision.

In May 1239, Brother Elias was removed as Minister General, a move which limited subsequent efforts to spread this form of life to other houses. Pope Gregory himself presided over the chapter of the brothers and it seems likely that Elias's exertions on Clare's behalf contributed to his ouster. The Order of Lesser Brothers was now led by friars who were trying to limit their pastoral responsibilities toward female houses and were thereby not interested in spreading the *forma vivendi* embraced by the San Damiano model. Although now assigned to minister to the sisters in Cortona, Elias may have continued to encourage other women to adopt San Damiano's way of life. According to Thomas of Eccleston, the pope eventually excommunicated the former General Minister because he continued to visit the Poor Ladies (*pauperes dominae*) – Gregory's name for the Damianite sisters – without permission.[121] Clare became very ill at this time and her interests came to focus primarily on preserving her own community's vision of radical poverty. With Elias in exile, those sisters who were committed to this early form of life were left without allies among the leadership of the Lesser Brothers, a circumstance which may have contributed to the growth of the phenomenon of the *sorores minores*, the Minoresses.[122]

In the first few decades of the thirteenth century, the sources use this term to refer to the small groups of penitent women who shared a symbiotic existence with the Lesser Brothers (*Sorores Minores* being the analogue of *Fratres Minores*).[123] There are obvious similarities be-

---

[121] Cited in Maria Pia Alberzoni, "Sorores Minores e autorità ecclesiastica fino al pontificato di Urbano IV," in *Chiara e la diffusione delle clarisse del secolo XIII: atti del Convegno di studi in occasione dell=VIII Centenario della nascita di Santa Chiara. Manduria, 14-15 dicembre 1994*, ed. Giancarlo Andenna and Benedetto Vetere (Galatina: Congedo, 1998), 181-82 [English translation: "*Sorores minores* and Ecclesiastical Authority as far as the Pontificate of Urban IV," in *Clare of Assisi and the Poor Sisters*, 125].

[122] The *sorores minores* (also called *minoretae*) have, unfortunately, often been overlooked in studies on Clare. For the phenomenon see Alberzoni, "*Sorores minores*," 114-53; Optatus van Osseldonk, "*Sorores Minores*. Una nuova impostazione del problema," *Collectanea Franciscana* 62 (1992): 595-634.

[123] The earliest reference is Jacques de Vitry's famous description of the penitential movement from 1216 (see Armstrong, *The Lady*, 428). Francis supposedly rejected this term. Thomas of Pavia recorded an anecdote in which Francis told Cardinal Hugolino that the women entrusted to the brothers' care should not be called the lesser sisters (*sorores minores*) but rather ladies (*dominae*); see FA:ED 3, 794. These examples should not suggest that there was a standard use of the name. The identifica-

tween these Minoresses and the sisters at San Damiano, although the former were less likely to live in fixed communities. It is therefore unlikely that Clare or San Damiano represented an institutional model for them. Throughout the 1230s, some communities of the Minoresses were regularized as a part of the Order of San Damiano. Others were able to remain more or less independent with the support of sympathetic friars like Elias. By the beginning of the 1240s, however, the Minoresses became the targets of the pope's increasingly antagonistic approach to alternative models of women who were choosing to follow Francis.

In 1241 Pope Gregory issued a bull protesting the claims of certain *Minoretae* who were claiming falsely to be members of the Order of San Damiano.[124] They wore the Damianite habit and sandals in place of shoes but how could they be Damianites, the pope protested, when they did not live in enclosed communities. He thus directed the bishops who received the bull to compel the women to abandon the Damianite habit. This condemnation clearly reveals the pope's irritation. He had been working to regularize women's religious life for almost a quarter century and here were women not only challenging his efforts, but even claiming to be members of an order he had instituted. He also expressed his concern that the faithful might think these women really were Damianites, thus bringing scandal to that order and to their brothers, who were their pastoral ministers.

His successor, Innocent IV, issued similar bulls condemning the *sorores minores* twice during 1246 and again in 1250, 1251, and 1257.[125] He adds an interesting detail describing the Minoresses' way of life:

---

tion appears infrequently in the early narrative sources and, as Alberzoni has noted, it appears only "by negation" in the notarial documents – that is, when a community was closed or transferred to an established order. This lack of documents makes it very difficult to assess the number of Minoresses or their communities. See Alberzoni, "*Sorores minores*," 124.

[124] *Bullarium Franciscanum* I, 290.

[125] The 1250 bull is published in *Bullarium Franciscanum* I, 541, see *Bullarium Franciscanum* II, 83-84 for the 1257 edition. The 1246 bull is edited by Maria Pia Alberzoni in "Il francescanesimino femminile in Lombardia fino all'introduzione della regola urbaniana," in *Chiara e il secondo Ordine: il fenomeno francescano femminile nel Salento: atti del Convegno di studi in occasione dell'VIII centenario della nascita di Santa Chiara: Nardò, 12-13 novembre 1993* (Galatina: Congedo, 1997), 219-20. These bulls were primarily addressed to bishops in central and northern Italy as well as southern France, but one of the 1251 bulls was addressed to the prelates of England.

they were *vagantes*. Rather than living in fixed communities as the Damianite Constitution required, they traveled about various regions unlike proper religious women who lived in a strict enclosure. His tone was considerably harsher than Gregory's, reflecting the degree to which the *sorores minores* had become a problem. Pope Gregory's condemnation seems to have originated in part from the brothers' request to limit these group's claims on the Order of St. Damian. Innocent IV's bulls add that these women were making (improper) claims on the Lesser Brothers. The demands of the *cura monialium*, however, are an insufficient explanation for the controversial status of the minoresses.[126] Scholars have recognized that there seems to have been a dissident movement by some women – identified as *sorores minores* – to preserve an earlier penitential form of life in which the sisters lived in the manner of the early brothers. In the 1240s there is no evidence to connect these women directly to Clare or to San Damiano, which had always been a stable community for the women. It is worth noting that she did not use the name *sorores minores* in her rule, but rather identified her followers as the Order of Poor Sisters.[127] Indeed, none of the bulls condemning the Minoresses indicate that evangelical poverty was a critical aspect of their lives as it had been for Clare.

Thus, through the 1240s the development of institutional female forms of life in Italy was less uniform and systematic than tradition recognizes. It had three distinct forms: Clarian (San Damiano and a few closely connected houses who followed Francis's *forma vivendi* or had an exemption for radical poverty), Damianite (enclosed communities who professed the Hugolinian Constitution),[128] and the *Sorores Minores* (non-cloistered women loosely inspired by Francis, whose lives were governed by custom, rather than formal statutes). Certainly there were similarities between the three groups, most notably by a desire in the

---

[126] In 1245 the Franciscan General Minister petitioned the pope to relieve the Order of its responsibility to enclosed women. His request was denied and the pope incorporated fourteen new communities into the Order of San Damiano, for which the friars were responsible. He conceded, however, that the Friars would be allowed to approve any further new communities; see *Bullarium Franciscanum* I, 420.

[127] Isabelle of France preferred that title *sorores minores* for the sisters governed by her rule, but she too had to negotiate its negative connotation for the papal curia and Lesser Brothers.

[128] This does not indicate uniformity of observance since his rule existed in three different redactions (1219, 1228, and 1239 – a house could follow an earlier version), and many houses had individual exemptions.

1240s for a connection with the Lesser Brothers. Pope Innocent IV recognized this point and used it to promote his own legislation for the female order.

Shortly after his election to the papacy,[129] he reconfirmed the Hugolinian Constitutions, but soon decided to issue his own rule. It diverged in three key ways from the earlier legislation.[130] First, in response to concerns from the women, he removed all references to the Benedictine Rule and in their place he established Francis's form of life for San Damiano (*beati Francisci regula*) as the basis of their observance. This may seem to be a concession to Clare and her followers. However, the pope's motivation was to link the papal order defined by the Hugolinian constitutions with Francis as a reproof to the Minoresses for claiming a privileged relationship with the Lesser Brothers.[131] Second, he clarified their connections to the Lesser Brothers, for example by having the sisters follow their liturgical customs and requiring that the visitator be a Lesser Brother. Third, Innocent's rule called for greater oversight generally by the brothers – the abbess' election had to be confirmed by the General Minister or Provincial and approval of the General Chapter of the Lesser Brothers was necessary before a new community could be established. These additions reflect a tendency which Innocent shared with Gregory IX toward regularizing female religious life through increased clerical authority.[132] Indeed, one of the reasons his rule was not widely accepted was that it took away individual autonomy from each house. Giovanna Casagrande proposes that the relative openness of Hugolino's constitution made it more appealing to many communities.[133] Clare, of course, objected to the provision that each community hold communal property. At this time, she began to think about expanding Francis's *forma vivendi* into

---

[129] *Bullarium Franciscanum* I, 394.

[130] *Bullarium Franciscanum* I, 476-83; English translation in Armstrong, *The Lady*, 89-105. In common with the Hugolinian Constitutions, Innocent's rule mandated that houses own property.

[131] Compare Alberzoni, "Sorores minores," 128. Innocent's rule also made clear that Francis's form of life was binding only for the traditional monastic vow of obedience, poverty, and chastity (see FLInn 1).

[132] Mueller also connects these efforts as a part of the expanding claims of papal authority (against the backdrop of the papal-imperial conflict). See *The Privilege of Poverty*, 89.

[133] Giovanna Casagrande, "La regola di Innocenzo IV," in *Clara claris praeclara*, 71-82.

a more formal rule that also reflected how life at San Damiano had developed in the two decades since his death.[134]

Given the papal curia's concerns about dissident forms of the manner in which women applied Francis's vision, it seems remarkable that Innocent approved Clare's rule. The two had no previous personal connection, unlike Pope Gregory and Clare. In fact, Innocent probably met her only when he came to San Damiano for the first time just prior to her death.[135] He certainly knew that she wanted his confirmation of her *forma vitae* and the *Privilege of Poverty*, but his knowledge of her friction with his predecessor had led him to delay making a decision. Now, buoyed by Cardinal Rainaldo's reassurances and finding Clare to be a humble and devout woman, he approved her rule.[136]

This would, however, be an underestimation of Clare. Her rule, after all, begins with the statement that it is the form of life of the Order of the Poor Ladies (FLCl 1:1), a clear declaration that she and her followers were not a part of the papal Order of San Damiano. Her frequent references to Francis, the Lesser Brothers, and their customs – not to mention the text's resemblance to the *Later Rule* – make clear that this was a document connected to Francis. The identification of the Order of Poor Sisters is the principal evidence that her ambitions extended to communities beyond her own house.[137] Nevertheless, there is little evidence that other communities of women sought to adopt her *forma vitae* outside Agnes of Prague's foundation. Some scholars have suggested that other houses in the Spoleto Valley with close ties to Clare's community also professed her rule, but

---

[134] The traditional range of dates for the composition of Clare's *forma vitae* begins with the promulgation of Innocent IV's rule on August 6, 1247 (*Bullarium Franciscanum* I, 476-83). It ends with Cardinal Rainaldo de' Segni's approval of Clare's *forma vitae* on September 16, 1252.

[135] For their relationship, see Alberzoni, "Clare and the Papacy," 57-61.

[136] As a trained canonist, Pope Innocent may have viewed her rule more as a source of spiritual direction than a juridical document that would have "competed" with the papal legislation.

[137] Scholars have cited several other passages as evidence that Clare was thinking of a confederation of houses, not simply her own community (or even the network of houses in the Spoleto Valley plus Saint Francis in Prague). The references to the Cardinal Protector and Franciscan General Minister (e.g. FLCl 4:12) could indicate a desire to spread the rule to other communities. Also, the allowance that the abbess could modify the sisters' dress as the location or season dictates (FLCl 2:16) allows for Clarian practices in places outside central Italy. See Federazione, *Una vita prende forma*, 109.

no presently known document or manuscript confirm this assumption. Even Clare's own community soon renounced her rule. In 1257, the sisters left San Damiano for a safer location within Assisi's town wall, settling in a new convent which they named Santa Chiara. Presumably they were still following Clare's *forma vitae* since its observance was reconfirmed in 1266.[138] However, not long afterwards the women were allowed to inherit or buy property and had become "Urbanists" in practice by 1288.[139]

Thus, one of the most significant problems in identifying Clare as the leader of a poverty movement whose vocational choice was validated in her *forma vitae* is to explain why the movement effectively disappears shortly after her death. The suppression of her rule and personal charism through the generic portrait in her hagiographical legends were contributing factors. The efforts of the surviving members of the Early Lesser Brothers (Leo and others) also were too limited. But if the early female movement is not Clare-centered as a history of the order's institutionalization confirms, it becomes easier to see why most women favored one of the papal rules. These statutes supported their goal of a formal relationship with the Lesser Brothers, without the extreme poverty of her *forma vitae*.[140] The female movement, thus, became tied more to the Lesser Brothers than to Clare.

Most of the unresolved questions concerning the *Rule of Saint Clare* arise from its later history after the years of Clare's life, as this chapter already has suggested. Certainly, the most pressing issue is to better understand what happened to Clare's rule or *forma vitae* between the middle of the thirteenth century and its rediscovery by Observant Reformers in the later Middle Ages. Looking more closely at the manuscripts of the rule will contribute to a greater understanding of its transmission. The Protomonastery in Assisi is the obvious starting place, but other Clarissan communities whose archives have re-

---

[138] *Bullarium Franciscanum* III, 107. Stefano Brufani has commented on the irony of this exemption – the sisters in Assisi were rejecting their membership in the Order of Saint Clare! See "La Memoria di Chiara d'Assisi," in *Clara Claris Praeclara*, 501-23.

[139] See *Bullarium Franciscanum* IV, 26.

[140] See Knox, "Audacious Nuns," 54-62.

ceived less attention may yet reveal surprising discoveries.[141] Of the six Latin manuscripts of the *Rule of Saint Clare* used to produce the most recent critical edition, three are still held in convent libraries (Assisi, Messina, and Urbino). Other houses connected with the Observant Reform movement may reveal additional discoveries.[142]

Such an investigation also will reveal new information about vernacular versions of the rule, a subject which has received very little attention. How did these texts circulate and where were they produced? It would be interesting to know whether there is a "standard" translation of the rule within the different vernacular traditions. Are these translations literal, or are they more liberal with added or deleted passages reflecting the sisters' concerns? Recent research on the vernacular translations of the *Legend of Saint Clare*, a text which also circulated widely through reformed communities, has shown how Clare's image and authority changed over time and according to its audience.[143] Are there parallel examples in the translations of her rule? It would be helpful to have a census of these documents – where do copies survive and in what numbers?

These late medieval copies of the *Rule of Saint Clare* were often accompanied by a commentary, as the Urbino manuscript demonstrated. These commentaries are not well known. John of Capistrano's *Declaratio* was probably the best known of these texts due to his prominence, but Nicholas of Osimo also wrote one which circulated among the women.[144] By the start of the sixteenth century the Clarisses were writ-

---

[141] Compare Michael Bihl, ed. "Documenta inedita archivi Protomonasteri S. Clarae Assisi," *Archivum Franciscanum Historicum* 5 (1912): 291-98; Robinson, "Inventarium omnium documentorum," *Archivum Franciscanum Historicum* 1 (1908): 413-32.

[142] Among the reform communities, Monteluce has received the most attention thanks to its detailed chronicle and rich archive of documents, many of which are now in the Biblioteca Comunale Augusta in Perugia. See, for example, Ignazio Baldelli, "Codice e carte di Monteluce," *Archivio italiano per la storia della pietà* 1 (1951): 387-93; Stefano Felicetti, "Aspetti e risvolti di vita quotidiana in un monastero Perugino riformata: Monteluce, secolo XV," *Collectanea Franciscana* 65 (1995): 553-642; and now Umiker, "Il volgarizzamento."

[143] The Italian tradition has received more attention than other vernaculars thanks to the work of Giovanni Boccali, among others. See his working manuscript census in "Tradizione manoscritta delle legende di Santa Chiara di Assisi," in *Clara Claris Praeclara*, 419-501.

[144] See Lucio M. Nuñez, ed. "Explicatio Regulae S. Clarae auctore Fr. Nicolao de Auximo O.F.M. (1446) deque alia auctore S. Ioanne de Capistrano (1445)," *Archivum Franciscanum Historicum* 5 (1912): 299-314.

ing their own commentaries, although they do not seem to have circulated as widely. For example, Battista da Varano's *Dechiarazione sopra i capituli de le sore povere de Santa Chiara*, which survives in an unique manuscript in her former convent of Santa Chiara in Camerino, is a vernacular adaptation of John of Capistrano's commentary.[145] The manuscript tradition of these commentaries also needs to be studied, as does the relationship between the different texts.

These codicological investigations can help lay the groundwork for a cultural history of the *Rule of Saint Clare*. For example, we would like to know more about what was known about the rule during those years when it was "lost." Those who knew Clare of Assisi primarily through the bull of canonization or one of the thirteenth-century hagiographical legends would not have known that she wrote a religious rule or that Pope Innocent IV had approved it. Francis's own *legendae* briefly refer to Clare and her community, of course, but not to his *forma vivendi* for San Damiano.[146] Nonetheless there are intriguing references to indicate that knowledge of Clare's *forma vitae* survived in some circles. Marco Bartoli has proposed the existence of a "San Damiano cycle," referring to her community's role in preserving the memory of the early day of the Lesser Brothers.[147] This might account for Ubertino of Casale's knowledge that the sisters had a rule other than the Urbanist one, or Angelo of Clareno's belief that Clare was excommunicated by Pope Gregory IX for refusing to accept property for

---

[145] Camilla Battista da Varano, *Le Opere Spirituali*, ed. Giacomo Boccanera (Jesi: Scuola Tipografia Francescana, 1958), 265-302. A seventeenth-century Clarisse, Maria Domitilla Galuzzi also wrote a commentary, see E. Ann Matter, "The Canon of Religious Life: Maria Domitilla Galluzzi and the *Rule* of Clare of Assisi," in *Strong Voices, Weak History: Early Women Writers in England, France, and Italy*, ed. Pamela Joseph Benson and Victoria Kirkham (Ann Arbor: University of Michigan Press, 2005), 78-98.

[146] Compare 2C 204 which only notes Francis's promise that his successors would minister to San Damiano. Jacques Dalarun has shown that even the praise for Clare in Thomas's earlier biography is really directed at the Order of San Damiano. See his *La Malaventura di Francesco d'Assisi. Per un uso storico delle leggende francescane* (Milan: Edizioni Biblioteca Francescana, 1996), 52-61. [English: *The Misadventure of Francis of Assisi* (St. Bonaventure, NY: Franciscan Institute Publications, 2002), 75-88.]

[147] Marco Bartoli, "Novitas Clariana. Chiara testimone di Francesco," in *Chiara d'Assisi: Atti del XX Convegno internazionale* (Spoleto: Centro italiano di studi sull'alto medioevo, 1993), 157-85. For criticism of this idea, see Dalarun, *The Misadventure*, 81-88.

San Damiano.[148] These or other Spiritual Franciscans may have been the conduit for Queen Sancia of Mallorca's knowledge of the *Rule of Saint Clare*. One wonders whether there was much debate in the papal curia over Clare's request that her communities beyond San Damiano be allowed to profess her earlier rule. To what extent was Clare's *forma vitae* still a provocative text? How did its reputation change over time and according to interest?

Finally, we also need to explore further differences in how the brothers and sisters understood what it meant for the women to return to their "first rule."[149] Mariano of Florence proclaimed without any intended irony that the sisters' return to their primary legislation defined good reform: "all ... lived under the rule which Saint Clare received from Saint Francis, in the highest poverty like the Lesser Brothers, and with the aforementioned modifications of Pope Eugene."[150] John of Capistrano's rule commentary explained the standard of observance from his perspective. His decrees on enclosure, pastoral care, individual poverty, fasting and silence all reflect a standard ecclesiastical view of enclosed female life. It hardly varied from the Urbanist rule that had governed most houses for the past two centuries, suggesting that Clare's *forma vitae* had been neutralized.[151] Stories told by the women, however, demonstrate how they often resisted moderations to the *Rule of Saint Clare* because they had responded to its original intentions, including a more literal interpretation of her *forma vitae* including its strict standards of poverty. Clare's charismatic status as foundress of the female Order derives from the interest of these women in her struggles to define a female way to follow Francis's way of life. Scholars are beginning to pay more attention to stories of these women, not only moderated through chroniclers like Fra Mariano, but

---

[148] See Gian Luca Potestà, *Angelo Clareno: dai poveri eremiti ai fraticelli* (Rome: Istituto storico italiano per il Medio Evo, 1990), 267-68.

[149] For some preliminary reflections, see Knox, "One and the Same Spirit," 11-22.

[150] Mariano, *Libro delle degnità*, paragraph 91. Pope Eugene's modifications refer to relaxation of the standard of poverty, including endowments for the sisters.

[151] It is striking that the chapter which receives the shortest commentary is chapter six where Clare recounted her vocation for apostolic poverty. His lack of comment thus seems to indicate little concern for her spiritual motivation or mutual charism with the brothers. Outside a reference to Francis's promise of perpetual care in his comments on the rule's first chapter, John only refers to Clare in the sisters' vow of profession (a text which had been borrowed from the Urbanist Rule).

also to those found in their own chronicles, spiritual treatises, and *vitae*.[152] These texts will provide important information about how the sisters understood their own religious identity, including how the *Rule of Saint Clare* shaped it.

III. INTERPRETING THE TEXT

a) Structure

The *Rule of Saint Clare* was divided into twelve chapters so as to clarify its textual dependence on Francis's *Later Rule*. The correlation between the two Franciscan rules is not precise, however, nor can the structure of Clare's *forma vitae* be explained entirely through reference to the earlier papal constitutions.[153] This diversity raises the question of how Clare and her collaborators originally conceived of its organization. A close examination of the text suggests an internal logic underlying the sometimes artificial groupings created by the chapters. The *Rule of Saint Clare* opens with a statement of the sisters' identity (FLCl 1), moves to entrance and formation (FLCl 2), regulations for daily life (FLCl 3-10), internal governance (FLCl 11), and then concludes with relations with the external world, including the role of the Cardinal Protector and the responsibilities of the Friars Minor (FLCl 12). As Jean François Godet-Calogeras has noted, this organization at its broadest level represents the stages of the sisters' formation in reli-

---

[152] Lezlie S. Knox, *Creating Clare of Assisi: Female Franciscan Identities in Later Medieval Italy* (Leiden: Brill, 2008), 157-86 esp. Intriguing discoveries are emerging for the convent of Montevergine in Messina, home to the famous codex. A dissertation in progress at the University of California, Santa Barbara is looking at the sisters' intellectual activities, see Jessica Weiss, "Convent as Classroom: the Education of Women in Renaissance Italy," PhD Dissertation, 2010x). See also Donatella Lisciotto, "Suor Jacopa Pollicino Clarissa," Collectanea Franciscana 79 (2009): 627-40. For the intellectual culture in convents more broadly, see Kate Lowe, *Nuns' Chronicles and Convent Culture in Renaissance and Counter Reformation Italy* (Cambridge: Cambridge University Press, 2003); Anne Winston-Allen, *Convent Chronicles: Women Writing about Women and Reform in the Late Middle Ages* (University Park, PA: Pennsylvania State University Press, 2004).

[153] The structure of these rules can be easily compared by reviewing the different chapter titles. There is a useful chart listing them in Carney, *The First Franciscan Woman*, 260-61.

gious life. [154] Certainly, the flow of the text appears rather disjointed in places, as the tone can shift awkwardly between juridical demands and more personal remarks. For example, chapter two jumps from a formal requirement that only professed sisters live in the community to a fervent appeal by Clare that the sisters always dress in simple clothing following the example of the Poor Christ (FLCl 2:23-24). [155] Such interjections, along with other personal reflections, reveal how Clare understood her text to be not just a legislative document (a *regula*) but also a spiritual testimony to her vision of life (a *forma vitae*). This perspective emerges more directly by considering the major themes in the text.

b) Themes, symbols, images

Compared to Clare's other writings, there is less development of religious imagery or symbolism in this document. [156] This characterization is hardly surprising since the function of a religious constitution is to define, for example, where, when and what the sisters pray more than to meditate on the practice of contemplative prayer. [157] But as stated above, Clare's *forma vitae* was as a hybrid text – both rule and spiritual guide. In the latter mode, it presents a fundamental declaration about the sisters' spiritual identity: they are living out the gospel form of life based on their love of the Poor Christ (FLCl 1:2). Poverty is obviously a key component to their evangelical charism, as her autobiographical reflections in what became the sixth chapter make

---

[154] Godet-Calogeras, "Form of Life of Clare," 4-7. He also addressed this idea in an earlier article, "Progetto evangelico di Chiara oggi," *Vita Minorum* 56 (1985): 198-301.

[155] The previous passage was taken from Francis's *Later Rule* 2:15-16, but it also reflected a canonical requirement in the thirteenth century as the papal curia increasingly mandated that female houses be enclosed and exclude the laity from the cloister. It was common throughout the Middle Ages for noble women to live in religious houses either as children or widows. On the emphasis on enclosure, see Elizabeth Makowski, *Canon Law and Cloistered Women: Periculoso and Its Commentators 1298-1545* (Washington, DC: Catholic University of America Press, 1997).

[156] An excellent introduction to Clare's use of imagery is Catherine Mooney, "*Imitatio Christi* or *Imitatio Mariae*? Clare of Assisi and Her Interpreters," in *Gendered Voices: Medieval Saints and Their Interpreters*, ed. Catherine Mooney (Philadelphia: University of Pennsylvania Press, 1999), 52-77.

[157] Compare the requirements for liturgical prayer (FLCl 3:1-7) with her development of the mirror of contemplation in her third letter to Agnes of Prague.

clear. The subsequent passages develop the theological foundation to this ideal. Clare defines the sisters' labor as a blend of active work with their hands and the contemplative labor of devotion (FLCl 7:1-3). She then explains that the sisters do this work in order to serve the Lord in the highest form of humility and poverty (FLCl 8:1-6).[158] This part of the rule closely follows Francis's *Later Rule*, thus underscoring the ideal of *minoritas* – humility in all things – in her rule.[159]

The evangelical character of the *Rule of Saint Clare* has attracted much attention, particularly among contemporary Clares who are concerned with what it means to live out the tradition.[160] But the topic also has interested other scholars because it encapsulates the key institutional problem worked out in the *Rule of Saint Clare*: how can an evangelical charism be combined with life in a fixed community? Some scholars have argued over whether Clare had sought to live a more active life like the early friars until she was forced into strict enclosure by Pope Gregory IX, but this debate misses that her rule clearly states that the women were living a distinctly Franciscan way of life.[161] The sisters had been chosen by Francis, and, just as with the Early Brotherhood

---

[158] Clare here appropriated Francis's *Later Rule*, which makes clear that the Franciscans adopt radical poverty for the love of Christ and his mother (and addition by Clare); see LR 6:1-6.

[159] For further discussion, see Maria Pia Alberzoni, "Chiara d'Assisi: il carisma controverso," in *Charisma und religiöse Gemeinshaften im Mittelalter.* Akten des 3. Internationalen Kongresses des Italienisch-deutschen Zentrums für Vergleichende Ordensgeschichte (Münster: LIT, 2005), 319-42; Marco Bartoli, "La minorità in Chiara d'Assisi," in *"Minores et subditi omnibus." Tratti caraterizzanti dell'identità francescana: atti del Convegno, Roma, 26-27 novembre 2002*, ed. Luigi Padovese (Rome: 2003), 205-16.

[160] For example, Chiara Agnese Acquadro and Chiara Christiana Mondonico, "La Regola di Chiara di Assisi: Il Vangelo come forma di vita," in *Clara claris praeclara*, 147-232. These women are a part of the Franciscan research team whose most recent volume includes an extended commentary informed by historical analysis, see Federazione di S. Chiara, *Il Vangelo*, 73-490. Many modern commentaries on Clare's rule are concerned with this issue (reflecting Vatican II's call for religious orders to reengage with their founding charisms); see for example Javier Garrido, *La Forma de vida de Sancta Clara* (Aramzazu: Aldecoa Diego de Siloe, 1979). Carney addresses his insights concerning how the rule may be read as a series of exhortations to a deeper relationship with God, see *The First Franciscan Woman*, 90-91, and her own commentary on the contemporary meanings of the rule, 217-39.

[161] The theme of whether Clare wanted (in traditional monastic terms) the *vita activa* or the *vita contemplativa*, runs through Clarian studies. For a brief summary, see Christian-Frederik Falskau, *"Hoc est quod cupio*: Approaching the Religious Goals of Clare of Assisi, Agnes of Bohemia, and Isabelle of France," *Magistra* 12 (2006): 7-9.

he had established their way of life (FLCl 1:1-6, FLCl 6:1-10). The research team of Italian Clarisses have brought these elements together in noting that the Rule demonstrates how the evangelical charism was represented both in the person of Clare and in the historical development of the lives of the sisters at San Damiano.[162]

c) Significance of the Text

Hopefully, the richness of the text and history surrounding Clare's *forma vitae*, as discussed in this essay, have deepened its reputation as the first female-authored rule to receive papal sanction. (Does that claim now seem more a piece of trivia than a statement of significance?) The document that is now known as *The Rule of Saint Clare* represents her vision of female religious life: a democratic community shaped by its commitment to radical poverty and lived in a symbiotic relationship with the Lesser Brothers. It represents her commitment to these ideals as well as her willingness to fight for them both through direct confrontation and subtle modifications of her canonical sources. While this text had a limited circulation in the thirteenth century, Clare nonetheless played a significant role in the debates over the way her vision would take shape.

The Rule of Saint Clare itself played an equally important role two centuries later, when the sisters' identity as reformed Clarisses was linked to profession of their "first rule." These women did not think of her as author of the text: credit goes to Francis, as Clare – his "little plant" (FLCl 1:3) – intended. However, they recognized her spiritual authority and set about reclaiming Clare as a role model for the way they were to live their life. From this point onward, the *Rule of Saint Clare* became an integral part of the historical memory of Clare of Assisi.

---

[162] Acquadro and Mondonico, *Clara claris praeclara*, 150.

IV. BIBLIOGRAPHY

Manuscript tradition[163] and Editions

Assisi, Protomonastery of St. Clare (no shelf number), 1253.

Boccali, Giovanni, ed. *Opuscula s. Francisci et scripta s. Clarae Assiensium*. Assisi: Biblioteca Francescana, 1978. [Reprinted in *Fontes Francescani*. Ed. Enrico Menestò, Stefano Brufani, and Giuseppe Cremascoli. Medioevo francescano 2. Assisi: Porziuncula, 1995.]

Claire d'Assise: Écrits, ed. Marie-France Becker, Jean-François Godet, and Thaddée Matura, *Sources Chrétiennes* n. 325. Paris: Éditions du Cerf, 1985.

Messina, Biblioteca del Monastero di Montevergine (no shelf number), c. 1260, ff. 1r-18v.

Regula et Constitutiones generales pro monialibus Ordinis Sanctae Clarae. Rome: Tipografia poliglotta "Cuore di Maria," 1930 (revised in 1941 and 1973).

Seraphicus legislationis textus originales. Quaracchi: Collegio di San Bonaventura, 1897.

Uppsala, Universitätsbibliotheck, cod. C 63, fourteenth century, ff. 176r-180r

Urbino, Biblioteca del Monastero di S. Chiara (no number), 15th century, ff. 2v- 11r

English Translation

Armstrong, Regis, trans. *Clare of Assisi: The Lady*. 3rd revised edition. New York: New City Press, 2006.

Studies

Alberzoni, Maria Pia. *Clare of Assisi and the Poor Sisters in the Thirteenth Century*. Jean François Godet-Calogeras, ed. St. Bonaventure, NY: Franciscan Institute Publications, 2004.

---

[163] This bibliography lists only the manuscripts used in the critical editions. For an expanded discussion of additional medieval manuscripts of the Rule of Saint Clare, see Federazione S. Chiara di Assisi, *Il Vangelo*, 40-64.

_____. "Curia Romana e Regolamentazione delle Damianite e delle Domeni-
cane." In *Regulae—Consuetudines—Statuta. Studi sulle fonti normative degli
oridini religiosi nei secoli centrali del Medioevo.* Atti del I e del II Seminario
internazionale di studio del Centro italo-tedesco di storia comparata degli ordini religiosi. Cristina Andenna and Gert Melville, eds. Münster:
LIT, 2005. 501-37.

Bartoli Langeli, Attilio. *Gli autografi di frate Francesco e di frate Leone.* Corpus Christianorum: Autographa Medii Aevi. Vol. 5. Turnhout: Brepols,
2000.

Carney, Margaret. *The First Franciscan Woman: Clare of Assisi and Her Form of
Life.* Quincy, IL: Franciscan Press, 1993; St. Bonaventure, NY: Franciscan Institute Publicaitons, 2007.

Ciccarelli, Diego. "Contributi alla recensione degli scritti di S. Chiara." *Miscellanea Francescana* 79 (1979): 347-74.

*Clara Claris Praeclara: L'esperienza cristiana e la memoria di Chiara d'Assisi in
occasione del 750 anniversario della morte.* Santa Maria degli Angeli-Assisi:
Edizioni Porziuncola, 2004.

Conti, Martino. *Introduzione e commento alla Regola di S. Chiara d'Assisi.* Assisi:
Porziuncola, 2002.

De Fontette, Micheline. *Les Religieuses à l'âge classique du droit canon: recherches
sur les structures juridiques des branches féminines des ordres.* Paris: J. Vrin,
1967. especially 128-51.

Falskau, Christian-Frederik. "*Hoc est quod cupio*: Approaching the Religious
Goals of Clare of Assisi, Agnes of Bohemia, and Isabelle of France." *Magistra* 12 (2006): 3-29.

Federazione delle Clarisse S. Chiara d'Assisi di Umbria-Sardegna. *Chiara di
Assisi e le sue fonti legislative: Sinossi cromatica.* Padua: Edizioni Messaggero, 2003.

_____. *Chiara di Assisi: una vita prende forma: iter storico.* Padua: Edizioni Mes-
saggero, 2005.

_____. *Il Vangelo come forma di vita: in ascolto di Chiara nella sua Regola.*
Padua: Edizioni Messaggero, 2007.

Gennaro, Clara. "Il francescanesimo femminile nel XIII ecolo." *Rivista di storia e letteratura religiosa* 25 (1989): 259-80.

Grau, Engelbert. "Die Regel der hl. Klara (1253) in ihrer Abhängigkeit von der Regel der Mindenbrüder." *Franziskanische Studien* 35 (1953): 211-71.

Iriarte, Lazaró. *Letra y espíritu de la Regla de Santa Clara.* Valencia: Selecciones de Franciscanismo, 1975.

Knox, Lezlie. "'One and the Same Spirit' (2 Cel 204): The Friars and Sisters in Spiritual Union." *Franciscan Studies* 64 (2006): 235-54.

Lainati, Chiara Augusta. "Le fonti riguardanti il secondo ordine francescano delle Sorelle Povere di Santa Chiara." *Forma Sororum* 23 (1986): 131-45 and 196-220.

Marini, Alfonso. "'Ancilla Christi, Plantula sancti Francisci.' Gli scritti di Santa Chiara e la Regola." In *Chiara d'Assisi: Atti del XX Convegno,* 109-56.

Matter, Ann. "The Canon of Religious Life: Maria Domitilla Galluzzi and the *Rule* of Clare of Assisi." In *Strong Voices, Weak History: Early Women Writers in England, France, and Italy.* Pamela Joseph Benson and Victoria Kirkham, eds. Ann Arbor: University of Michigan Press, 2005. 78-98.

Mueller, Joan. *The Privilege of Poverty: Clare of Assisi, Agnes of Prague, and the Struggle for a Franciscan Ruler for Women.* University Park: Pennsylvania State University Press, 2006.

Oliger, Lucio. "De origine regularum Ordinis S. Clarae." *Archivum Franciscanum Historicum* 5 (1912): 181-209, 413-47 and 644-54.

Sensi, Mario. "Chiara d'Assisi nell'Umbria del Quattrocentro." *Collectanea Franciscana* 62 (1992): 163-87.

Umiker, Monica Benedetta. "Il volgarizzamento della "il Regola di S. Chiara" e le "Ordinazioni di Monteluce" secondo il ms. 25 della Chiesa Nuova in Assisi." *Archivum Franciscanum Historicum* 102 (2009): 174-226.

van Andrichem, Donatus. "Explicatio Primae Regulae S. Clarae auctore S. Ioanne Capistratensis (1445)." *Archivum Franciscanum Historicum* 22 (1929): 337-57 and 512-29.

The Testament of Clare

Michael W. Blastic

I. Establishing the Text

The *Testament* of Clare describes both the foundation of and the commitments for the way of life of the Poor Sisters of San Damiano. Foundationally, it describes the life that Clare and her sisters lived out in the turbulent years spanning their origin in 1211, with Clare's conversion, and continuing until her death in August of 1253. These final memories of Clare have been read by the Poor Clares from the thirteenth century. However, there are no early hagiographical references to the text, and until recently only vernacular editions of the text raised questions about its authenticity.

In the nineteenth century, Eduard Lempp first questioned the authenticity of Clare's *Testament*. His skepticism stemmed from the silence of the early sources,[1] and because of his belief that the Latin text available, that of Luke Wadding, used a Latin style that was too literal for someone untrained.[2] The Bollandist Francis Van Ortroy agreed with these arguments and also added another observation. He noticed a discrepancy between the *Testament* and the *Legend of the Three Companions* with regard to the origin of the Poor Ladies: the *Testament* pro-

---

[1] The *Testament* is not mentioned in the *Legend of Clare*, or the *Process of Canonization*, or in the *Bull of Canonization*. However, there are references to Clare entrusting the Privilege of Poverty to the sisters before her death (PC 3:32), which finds an echo in the text of the *Legend of Clare* 45, but without any mention of a final testament.

[2] Eduard Lempp, "Die Anfänge des Clarissenordens," *Zeitschrift für Kirchengeschichte* 13 (1892): 238-41.

poses that its juridical foundation came from Innocent III, while for
the *Three Companions* the origins are linked to Cardinal Hugolino.[3]

The argument for authenticity emerged in earnest in the twentieth
century. Paschal Robinson, who did some of the foundational early
textual research on Clare and the sisters, was the first to argue for its
authenticity in 1910.[4] Maria Fassbinder published a significant article
in 1936 defending the text's authenticity, despite the lack of hagiographical references and Latin manuscripts.[5] Englebert Grau, who has
written extensively on Clare and the Poor Ladies and who was initially
suspect of its authenticity, argued for its authenticity in 1979, and continued to sustain this position in his edition of Clare's writings.[6] The
arguments in favor of authenticity continued to develop throughout
the last century.[7]

The strongest argument presented against the authenticity of
Clare's *Testament* was the absence of any Latin manuscripts. Vernacular
editions of the text had been discovered, but until recently, the oldest
Latin edition was held to be that published by Luke Wadding in his
Annales Minorum. Wadding claimed to base his edition on an ancient
manuscript that he never described.[8] Wadding's text was copied by
the Bollandists and then published by the Franciscans at Quaracchi.[9]
However, since the *Testament* would have been read to the sisters during their meals, and given the unproven assumption that many of the
sisters would have been unable to understand Latin, it was simply as-

---

[3] Francis Van Ortroy, "La légende de s. François dite *Legenda trium sociorum*,"
Analecta Bollandiana 19 (1900): 128-31.

[4] Paschal Robinson, "The Writings of St. Clare of Assisi," *Archivum Franciscanum
Historicum* 3 (1910): 442-47.

[5] Maria Fassbinder, "Unterschungen über die Quellen zum Leben der hl. Klara
von Assisi," *Franziskanische Studien* 23 (1936): 296-306.

[6] Engelbert Grau, "Die Schriften der hl. Klara und die Werke ihrer Biographen,"
in *Movimento religioso femminile e francescanesimo nel secolo XIII*. Atti del VII Convegno
internazionale. Assisi, 11-13 ottobre 1979 (Assisi: Società internazionale di studi francescani, 1980), 195-238. Also see Englebert Grau, *Leben und Schriften der hl. Klara
von Assisi: Einführung, Übersetzung und Anmerkungen* (Werl: Dietrich-Coelde-Verlag,
1980), 1080.

[7] See the listing by Leonhard Lehmann, "La questione del Testamento di s. Chiara," in *Clara claris praeclara*. Atti del Convegno Internazionale. Assisi 20-22 novembre
2003 (Assisi: Edizioni Porziuncola, 2004), 258-59.

[8] Luke Wadding, *Annales Minorum*, ad anno 1253, nr. V.

[9] *Seraphicae Legislationis Textus originales* (Quaracchi: Collegium S. Bonaventurae,
1887), 272-80. The edition lacks verse forty-one of the text.

sumed that the text would have been translated very early from Latin into Italian and other vernaculars.[10] In fact, the vernacularization of the life and early history of the Poor Ladies by Mariano of Florence, published in 1519, included a vernacular edition of the *Testament* in his work.[11]

The first Latin manuscript discovered had been preserved in the Monastery of the Poor Clares of Montevergine in Messina, Sicily. Tradition held that this codex was found miraculously by Eustochia Calafato (1434-1485), the foundress of the Monastery of Montevergine. The sisters of Montevergine had a close relationship with the monastery of the Poor Clares of Monteluce in Perugia, which had a well respected scriptorium in the fifteenth and sixteenth centuries. From this scriptorium, it was believed, the Montevergine manuscript likely originated. Initially identified as a fifteenth century manuscript, this codex contains Clare's *Form of Life*, the Privilege of Innocent III (included as chapter thirteen of the *Form of Life*), the Papal Bull, *Solet annuere* of Innocent IV, September 9, 1253, the *Testament*, and Clare's *Blessing*. This codex was first described by Zefferino Lazzeri in 1950,[12] who then suggested the possibility that the manuscript might have been written by Brother Leo himself. This suggestion went unheeded until the recent work of Attilio Bartoli Langeli in 2000, who corrected the date of the codex as late thirteenth century.[13]

The second Latin manuscript of Urbino was discovered in 1957 by Fausta Casolini and described much later by Diego Ciccarelli.[14] This

---

[10] Ubaldo d'Alençon provides a listing of the vernacular manuscripts discovered, "Le plus ancien texte de la bénediction, du privilège de la pauvreté et du Testament de sainte Claire," *Revue d'Histoire Franciscaine* 1 (1924): 469-82.

[11] Mariano da Firezne, *Libro delle degnità et excellentie dell'Ordine della seraphica madre delle povere donne Sancta Chiara da Asisi*, ed. Giovanni Boccali (Assisi: Santa Maria degli Angeli, 1986), 44, 54, 123, 133.

[12] Zeffirino Lazzeri, "La *forma vitae* di s. Chiara a Messina?" *Chiara d'Assisi. Rassegna del Protomonastero* 2 (1950): 137-41. A more careful description of the codex, and its significance is provided by Diego Ciccarelli, "I manoscritti francescani della Biblioteca Universitaria di Messina," *Miscellanea Francescana* 78 (1978): 495-563, and "Contributi alla recensione degli scritti di s. Chiara," *Miscellanea Francescana* 79 (1979): 349-51.

[13] Attilio Bartoli Langeli, *Gli autografi di frate Francesco e frate Leone*. Corpus Christianorum, Autographa Medii Aevi, V (Belgium: Brepols, 2000), 104-30, which includes a photographic reproduction of the complete manuscript in Tables XII-XXVII.

[14] Fausta Casolini, "Origini del monastero fridericiano di s. Chiara in Urbino," *Chiara d'Assisi. Rassegna del Protomonastero* 5 (1957): 87-98. Ciccarelli, "Contributi," 352-53.

codex of parchment from the fifteenth century, contains Clare's *Forma vitae*, the bull of Innocent IV, and the *Testament* of Clare followed by her *Blessing*, both of which are in Latin and Italian. Another manuscript of paper from the fifteenth century was found to originate from this same monastery, containing Clare's *Forma vitae*, the *Testament* and her *Blessing*. The monastery of Urbino was founded in 1455 from the monastery of Monteluce in Perugia, again suggesting that both of these manuscripts might have originated from Monteluce.

A third Latin manuscript, from the Monastery of the Bridgetines in Vadstena, was discovered in 1970, and is also described by Ciccarelli.[15] Also judged to be from the fifteenth century,[16] it contains the *Rule of Innocent IV*, the privilege of Poverty of Innocent III, the *Forma vitae*, the *Testament* and the *Blessing* of Clare. The foundress of the monastery, Brigid of Vadstena, made a pilgrimage to Assisi, and so it is possible that the manuscript may have originated there.

A fourth Latin manuscript in the national Historical Archives of Madrid, is made up of two parts, the first part printed at Venice in 1500, and the second composed between the sixteenth and seventeenth centuries. Described by Angel Uribe in 1974, the second part contains the *Earlier Rule* of Francis, the *Forma vitae*, the *Testament* and *Blessing of Clare*, the Privilege of Poverty of Innocent III, and the *Rule* of Urban IV (1263).[17]

The critical edition of the *Testament* of Clare that was published in the *Sources chrétiennes* series, which formed the basis for the English translation in 1993 and 2006,[18] was based on these five manuscripts.[19] In an article published in the *Dizionario Francescano*, Chiara Lainati suggested that these five manuscripts used for this edition, all origi-

---

[15] Ciccarelli, "Contributi," 351. Also see, Henrik Roelvink, "Franciscan Elements in Two Libraries: Vadstena OssS and Stockholm OFM," in *A Catalogue and its Users: A Symposium on the Uppsala C Collection of Medieval Manuscripts*, ed. Monica Hedlund (Uppsala: Acta Universitatis Upsaliensis, 1985), 37-46.

[16] Grau, *Die Schriften der hl. Klara*," 214, note 63.

[17] Angel Uribe, "Nuevos escritos ineditos villacreacianos," *Archivo Ibero-Americano* 34 (1974): 303-34.

[18] *Clare of Assisi: Early Documents*. Revised and Expanded, translated by Regis J. Armstrong (St. Bonaventure, NY: Franciscan Institute Publications, 1993), and *Clare of Assisi: Early Documents. The Lady*, trans. Regis J. Armstrong (New York: New City Press, 2006).

[19] *Claire d'Assisi: Écrits*, ed. Marie-France Becker, Jean-François Godet and Thaddée Matura, Sources Chrétiennes 32 (Paris: Les Éditions du Cerf, 1985), 21-27.

nated from the scriptorium at Monteluce.[20] Thus, there was now a sufficient number of Latin manuscripts for providing a critical Latin edition of Clare's *Testament*, held now to be an authentic document that came from the bedside of Clare in the last days of her life.

In 1989, Giovanni Boccali published the description of another Latin manuscript from the Royal Albert Library of Brussels, ms. Lat. II. 1561, which was preserved at the College of St. Bonaventure at Grottaferrata in microfilm. Present in this codex was the *Forma vitae* of Clare, along with the bull of Innocent IV, the *Testament* followed by the *Blessing*, and a version of the vow formula in Flemish.[21] Boccali dated this manuscript in the fifteenth century and argued that it was very close to the manuscript from Uppsala. Based on this manuscript, plus the other five described above, Boccali published his own critical edition of the *Testament* and *Blessing* that is considered today to be the best.[22] Disagreeing with Lainati concerning the variants in the manuscripts, Boccali commented,

> Their collation and the presence of variant readings gives a trace of relationship among them, but not a dependence of one from the other, nor the possibility of their all originating from the same scriptorium, or from an immediate common original.... These few codices present an abundant number of variant readings. The testament has only ten verses that do not present variants, all the other verses have diverse readings, in particular the two central sections of the text (v. 17-31; 36-58).[23]

---

[20] Chiara Lainati, "Testamento di santa Chiara," *Dizionario Francescano*, ed. Ernesto Caroli (Padova: Messaggero, 1995), cols. 2049-2050. She comments that "With regard to the contents, rather, the variants do not represent any substantial changes," col. 2050.

[21] Giovanni Boccali, "Testamento e benedizione di s. Chiara. Nuovo codice Latino," *Archivum Franciscanum Historicum* 82 (1989): 273-305.

[22] Boccali's edition of the *Testament* and *Blessing* of Clare are included in the edition of Clare's writings published in the *Fontes Francescani*, ed. Enrico Menestò and Stfano Brufani (Assisi: Edizioni Porziuncola, 1995). However, the edition of the *Testament* and *Blessing* published in the *Sources Chrétiennes* edition of the writings is that used in the recent edition of Armstrong, *The Lady* (2006).

[23] Boccali, "Testament e benedizioni," 382.

Thus, the position holding a common origin of the text of the *Testament* to the scriptorium of the Monastery of Monteluce was dismissed.

At the International Symposium held in Assisi to celebrate the 750th anniversary of Clare's death in 1253, Leonhard Lehmann read a paper on Clare's *Testament* that argued for its authenticity.[24] Lehmann commented that, although the edition of Boccali placed the text of the *Testament* on a more secure base, it differed only a little from the proposal of the editors of the *Sources Chrétiennes* edition. However, at that point in 1982, with these five codices in addition to the printed edition of Wadding, the authenticity of the *Testament* was secure.

The authenticity came under question again with the investigation of Werner Maleczek in 1995.[25] Maleczek opened up the question of authenticity with a detailed analysis of the text of the *Privilege of Poverty* of Innocent III, purported to have been given to Clare in 1216.[26] Maleczek's main thesis, in short, was based on a "diplomatic" analysis of the text, and stated that, because the Privilege of Poverty of Innocent III did not follow the style or the norms of similar documents emanating from Innocent's curia, it had to be a forgery. The content of the text also raised questions, specifically in that it seemed not to fit with the status of the Poor Ladies in 1216.[27] He concluded that the

---

[24] Lehmann's essay was published together with the other papers given at the symposium in *Clara claris praelaris. Atti del Convegno Internazionale. L'esperienza cristiana e la memoria di Chiara d'Assisi in occasione del 750° anniversario della morte. Assisi 20-22 novembre 2003* (Assisi: Edizioni Porziuncola, 2004). This publication also appeared as the entire issue of *Convivium Assisiense* 6.2 (2004).

[25] Lehmann, "La questione del testamento di s. Chiara," 265. Lehmann mentions "five" codices, and counts the two manuscripts of Urbino as one.

[26] Werner Maleczek, "Das Privilegium Paupertatis Innocenz' III. und das Testament der Klara von Assisi. Überlegungen zur Frage ihrer Echtheit," *Collectanea Franciscana* 65 (1995): 5-82 [English Translation: "Questions about the Authenticity of the Privilege of Poverty of Innocent III and of the Testament of Clare of Assisi," *Greyfriars Review* 12 Supplement (1998): 1-80].

[27] Sentence 8 of this so-called *Privilege of Poverty* of Innocent III reads: "And if any woman does not wish to, or cannot observe a proposal of this sort, let her not have a dwelling place among you, but let her be transferred to another place." There are no indications that some of the sisters at San Damiano in 1216 were objecting to the poor life followed there. Text from, *Clare of Assisi: Early Documents*. Revised and Expanded, trans. and ed. by Regis Armstrong (St. Bonaventure, NY: Franciscan Institute Publications, 1993), 85-86. It is interesting to note that the text of this privilege is not contained in the recent edition of Armstrong's *The Lady* (2006).

Privilege of Poverty was a fifteenth century forgery originating in the context of the Observant Reform that sought to return the Poor Clares to the authentic ideals of Clare of Assisi. Maleczek traced this forgery to Central Italy, and specifically to Umbria, where the observant friars had a close relationship with the monastery of Monteluce in Perugia. Given the supposed dependence of the extant manuscripts at this time on the Urbino manuscript with its connection to Monteluce, as argued by Chiara Lainati, Maleczek believed that this monastery was the origin of the hoax.

Maleczek proceeded to point out similar inconsistencies and difficulties in Clare's *Testament*. Since there is a reference to Innocent III's privilege in her *Testament*,[28] this connection had for Maleczek the effect of guilt by association. Thus, the authenticity of the *Testament* was placed in doubt. In fact, in addition to the reference to the *Privilege of Poverty*, the *Testament* contained a similar reference to the possibility of the sisters leaving San Damiano for another place (v. 52), a situation which does not seem to fit within the context of the sisters at the time of Clare's death. It does make sense, however, a number of years later, when the Poor Ladies leave San Damiano for the monastery of Santa Chiara in the city of Assisi, and there continue the struggle against new attempts of the papacy to have them adopt the Rule of Urban IV.

Also, for Maleczek, the *Testament* recounts Francis's prophecy concerning San Damiano (vv. 13-14). Clare's *Testament* is an almost exact reproduction of Francis's words, purportedly spoken in French, as found in the *Legend of the Three Companions* (L3C 24), which appeared in 1246. Why would Clare, the obvious source of the story in the *Legend of the Three Companions*, retell the story at her death in a textually dependent manner? And, because the manuscripts that contain the Privilege also contain the *Testament* of Clare, this evidence gave further support to Maleczek's judgment of inauthenticity. The final straw for him was the dating of the extant manuscripts. At the time that Maleczek did his analysis of the texts (1995) there were no Latin manuscripts dated prior to the fifteenth century, with each of these manuscripts be-

---

[28] TestCl 42-43: "Moreover, for greater security, I took care to have our profession of the most holy poverty that we promised our father strengthened with privileges by the Lord Pope Innocent, in whose time we had our beginning, and by his other successors, that we would never in any way turn away from her." Armstrong, *The Lady*, 62.

ing related to the Monastery of Monteluce in Perugia the source of the forgery of the Privilege of Poverty. This, Maleczek believed, placed his conclusion of inauthenticity on a solid historical basis.

The reaction to Maleczek's argument was swift. Emore Paoli, who provided the introduction to the texts associated with Clare of Assisi in the *Fontes Francescani* published in 1995, concurred with his refutation of the Privilege of Poverty but only admitted that this made the *Testament* suspect at best. He suggested that the reference to the privilege in the *Testament* verse 42, did not refer to a document, but rather to a possible oral agreement between Innocent and Clare.[29] Niklaus Kuster attempted to refute the arguments of Maleczek point by point, but without adducing any new argument for its authenticity.[30] Maria Pia Alberzoni translated the German article of Maleczek into Italian, which was published in 1996, within a year of its original publication in

---

[29] Emore Paoli comments on verse 42-43 of the *Testament* and its context, "In reality, on the basis of the text, what can be concluded is only that Clare is preoccupied (*sollicita fui*) to proceed so that (*facere*) the profession of most holy poverty (*nostram professionem sanctissimae paupertatis*), the observance of which she together with her sisters are committed before God and Francis (*quam Domino et beato patri nosto promisimus*), be reinforced through privileges (*privilegiis … roborari*) from Innocent III and his successors (*a domino papa Innocentio … et aliis successoribus suis*) so that her community does not fall short, and would never fall short for any reason, of the profession they made (*ne aliquo tempore ab ipsa declinaremus ullatenus*)," *Fontes Francescani*, 2240. The *Legenda sanctae Clarae*, 14, suggests that "She asked a privilege of poverty from Innocent III of happy memory, desiring that her Order be known by the title of poverty," and goes on to say that Innocent wrote the first draft of the privilege with his own hand. Maleczek suggested that it would have been quite incredible for Clare to have a direct relationship with Innocent without a procurator. Paoli suggests that the episode referred to in the Legend is an "improbable hagiographical amplification" and highly unlikely given the operation of Innocent and his curia (2242). Michael Cusato has argued that in the light of Lateran IV's canon thirteen, Clare did need some sort of approval from the Pope for her form of life. He argues that this was given orally in 1216 with Francis as her spokesman, an approval similar to the original approval of the Lesser Brothers in 1209. Consult his article, "From the *Perfectio sancti Evangelii* to the *Sanctissima Vita et Paupetas*: An Hypothesis on the Origin of the *Privilegium Paupertatis* to Clare and Her Sisters at San Damiano," *Franciscan Studies* 64 (2006): 123-44.

[30] Niklaus Kuster, "Das Armutsprivileg Innocenz' III. und Klaras Testament: Echt oder raffinierte Fälschungen?" *Collectanea Franciscana* 66 (1996): 5-95. [English translation: "Clare's Testament and Innocent's Privilege of Poverty: Genuine or Clever Forgeries?" *Greyfriars Review* 15.2 (2001): 171-252.]

German.[31] The following year Alberzoni published an essay in which she supported the thesis of Maleczek regarding both the Privilege of Poverty and the *Testament*. This adduced further arguments for the position of inauthenticity.[32]

A decisive step in the general argument was taken by Attilio Bartoli Langeli in 2000, with his paleographical examination of the manuscript of Messina.[33] From his study, Bartoli Langeli concluded that the manuscript itself should be dated to the late thirteenth century. This earlier dating of the manuscript removed one of the strongest arguments of Maleczek for the inauthenticity of Clare's *Testament*, namely that no extant manuscripts of the *Testament* could be dated prior to the fifteenth century. While not resolving all the doubts concerning its authenticity, Bartoli Langeli's study showed that Clare's *Testament* stands on a surer footing.

In his study of the manuscript, Bartoli Langeli made a careful analysis of the script of the Messina manuscript. He compared this script with the autographs of Brother Leo on the *Chartula* and in Francis's *Breviary*, and arrived at the conclusion that the Messina manuscript was possibly written by Brother Leo. Given that he was present at San Damiano at Clare's death, Brother Leo would have been present for her final remarks to the sisters and brothers gathered at her bedside. Bartoli Langeli concluded that it is likely that Leo wrote this little book, the Messina codex, in the last years of his life. It was certainly written after Urban IV issued his Rule for the Poor Clares in 1264, because the Assisi monastery accepted that rule somewhat later. As Bartoli-Langeli comments:

> In the last years of his life brother Leo decided to leave books, the only way for him to perpetuate the memory of his heroes. The suspicion of manipulation which gravitates around the *Privilege of Poverty* and the *Testament* of Clare assumes, from

---

[31] *Chiara d'Assisi. La questione dell'autenticità del Privilegium Paupertatis e del Testamento*, trans. Maria Pia Alberzoni, Aleph, 14 (Milan: Editzione Biblioteca Francescana, 1996).

[32] Maria Pia Alberzoni, "San Damiano nel 1228. Contributo all "Questione clariana," *Collectanea Franciscana* 67 (1997): 459-77 [English translation: "San Damiano in 1228: A Contribution to the 'Clare Question,'" *Greyfriars Review* 13.1 (1999): 105-23].

[33] See footnote 13 above.

this point of view, an unexpected dimension. (Incidentally, one could ask whether a fifteenth century falsification would ever have been able to produce a little book such as this.) But it is not correct to adopt our critical categories of "authentic" and of "forgery," especially if brother Leo was its author and not only its scribe. This we hold most possible, as much as we are sure that his title of *authentic* interpreter of the actions, the words, and the will of Clare, as he was for Francis, cannot be taken from him.[34]

With the study by Bartoli Langeli, though questions still remained, the conclusion of the *Testament* of Clare as a forgery advanced by Maleczek and Alberzoni had lost much, if not all, of its weight.[35]

Accepting the role of Leo in the production of Clare's *Testament*, Leonhard Lehmann, in a 2003 symposium paper, addressed the question of the content of the *Testament*, and attempted to demonstrate its authenticity by comparing it with Clare's *Letters to Agnes*. In his work, Lehmann cited the study of Mario Marti,[36] as well as the study of Giovanni Pozzi and Beatrice Rima,[37] each of whom investigated the different styles utilized in the various writings of Clare. These scholars each concluded that the style of Clare's letters is that of the Roman Curia, a style of which Clare herself would have been incapable, since she left home too early to have developed it herself. Lehmann suggested that Clare had the help of a friar in the episcopal curia of Assisi to compose the *Letters to Agnes*. He argued however, that different from her letters to Agnes, Clare's *Testament* and *Blessing* preserved the spoken style of Clare, and that it was Leo who preserved this as well as the copies in

---

[34] Bartoli Langeli, *Gli autografi*, 128.

[35] Felice Accrocca, "L'illetterato e il suo testimone: considerazioni sull'autografia di frate Francesco e frate Leone in margine ad un recente volume," *Collectanea Franciscana* 72 (2002): 337-55, suggests that Bartoli Langeli's conclusions concerning Leo as the scribe might be overstated [English translation, "The 'Unlettered One' and His Witness: Footnotes to a Recent Volume on the Autographs of Brother Francis and Brother Leo," *Greyfriars Review* 16 (2002): 265-82].

[36] Mario Marti, "Sugli scritti di Santa Chiara d'Assisi," in *Ultimi contributi dal certo al vero, con bibliografia dell'autore*, ed. Mario Marti (Galatina: Congedo, 1995), 5-18.

[37] *Chiara d'Assisi, Lettere ad Agnese. La visione dello specchio*, ed. Giovanni Pozzi and Beatrice Rima (Milan: Adelphi, 1999). They do not study the style of Clare's *Testament* because they accepted Maleczek's conclusions.

the Messina codex.[38] Lehmann then proceeded to develop a concordance of ideas and expressions common to the *Letters to Agnes* and the *Testament*. On the basis of this concordance, Lehmann concluded to the authenticity of the *Testament*, as well as to brother Leo's role as scribe.[39]

In an introduction to a recent Italian edition of the writings of Clare published in 2004, Felice Accrocca presented a summary explanation of the status of her *Testament*.[40] In the work, Accrocca accepts the substantial authenticity of the *Testament* with some subsequent interpolations, and offers a working hypothesis to explain this. He suggests that the *Testament* does contain the essential memory of the admonitions which Clare gave to her sisters at the point of her death, as testified by Lady Filippa di Leonardo di Gislerio, the third witness for the *Process of Canonization*.[41] He hypothesizes that those memories were probably written down soon after her death. Then, some years later Brother Leo, who was present at the bedside of Clare at her death, was able to take up those written memories in order to sustain the companions and disciples of Saint Clare in their opposition to the attempt to introduce the Rule of Urban IV (1263).[42] Leo also interpolated other material into that written text of her words, and completed it with the prophecy of Francis (vv. 13-14) a story which would have been preserved by Clare and her sisters at San Damiano because of its intimate connection with their own vocation and which probably served as source of the story as it appeared in the *Legend of the Three Companions*.[43] Leo added the sentence about a possible abandonment

---

[38] Lehmann, "La questione del Testamento di s. Chiara," 270-79.

[39] Lehmann, "La questione del Testamento di s. Chiara," 293.

[40] *Chiara d'Assisi: La regola, le lettere, e il testamento spirituale. Tutti gli scritti della santa di Assisi*, intro. Felice Accrocca, trans. Modestino Cerra (Casale Monteferrato, Italy: Edizioni Piemme, 2004).

[41] PC III, 20-23, 33; Armstrong, *The Lady*, 160, 162.

[42] Accrocca describes the struggle of the sisters in Assisi to maintain their observance of Clare's *Form of Life* subsequent to the publication of Urban IV's Rule, and Leo's role in this struggle in "Chiara e l'Ordine Francescano," in *Clara claris praeclaris*, 350-54. He suggests that the Clare *Tavola*, c. 1280, rather than reflecting the Rule of Urban IV, emphasizes the observance of Clare's *Form of Life* especially through the episodes describing the origin of the sisters, as well as through the prominence that is given to the Friars Minor throughout the scenes, viewing it thus as an historical artifact that witnesses to this struggle.

[43] L3C 24. See below for Clare and her sisters as source for the story in later hagiography.

of San Damiano (v. 52), with Clare's invitation to her sisters to remain faithful to the ideal of poverty even in another place. It is not improbable, concludes Accrocca, that Leo was the scribe and compiler for the Messina manuscript, and thus the most important manuscript witness to the *Testament*.[44]

II. Approaching the Text

The Scriptures, especially those of the New Testament, serve as a primary source in all the writings attributed to Clare, and the *Testament* is no exception. The *Testament* of Clare, similar to that of Francis, reflects the genre of a biblical discourse of farewell.[45] One finds throughout the text allusions from Matthew and Luke, especially with regard to the human experience of Jesus from birth to death. Clare had direct access to the scriptures, together with the living experience of the texts as read, celebrated, and reflected on in the liturgy, and use of the biblical commentaries of the Fathers. Thus Clare and her sisters received the scriptures in a living, dynamic ecclesial-Franciscan context. The authors of a commentary on the *Testament* make this summary statement:

> The references to the Gospels are few but are given a fundamental character and they tell how the little plant reread in a personal manner the texts which form the basis of Francis's intuition; this holds also for the texts from the first letter of Peter (2:21).[46]

Given the working hypothesis of Felice Accrocca concerning the substantial authenticity of the *Testament* as the transcribed memory of Clare's last instructions and admonitions to her sisters, the appropriate historical context for these memories would be the situation of the Poor Ladies just prior to Clare's death and just prior to the approval of her *Form of Life* by Innocent IV. While yet waiting and hoping for the

---

[44] Accrocca, *Chiara d'Assisi*, 34-35.

[45] Giovanna Cremaschi and Agnese Acquadro, *Scritti di santa Chiara d'Assisi: Commento*, vol. I (Santa Maria degli Angeli: Edizioni Porziuncola, 1994), includes a section on the biblical sources of the *Testament*, 42-51.

[46] Cremaschi-Acquadro, *Scritti di santa Chiara d'Assisi*, 50.

papal approval, Clare reiterated the essential *iter* of the life of the Poor Sisters to that point.

Two elements stand out among her exhortations. The first is the repeated linkage of the life of the sisters with Francis and the brothers. The second element is the repeated insistence on fidelity to poverty. As Lady Phillipa di Leonardo di Ghislerio testified, "At the end of her life, after calling all her sisters, she entrusted the *Privilege of Poverty* to them."[47] These were the two elements of life that Clare struggled to maintain despite the efforts of the papacy and the curia to remove both from her form of life.

After reviewing the various arguments concerning the redaction and composition of the text, Alessandra Bartolomei Romagnoli concluded that the *Testament* of Clare is a "composite" text, woven with echoes and remembrances of Clare's words and from other early Franciscan documents. Romagnoli pointed to the text of the prophecy of Francis concerning the ladies who would come to dwell at San Damiano as an example. In addition, at the center of the *Testament*, there are texts cited from the *Form of Life* of Clare, chapter six, dealing with the writings left to Clare and the sisters by Francis.[48] Romagnoli goes on to suggest a working hypothesis similar to that of Accrocca. She writes,

> It is possible that after the death of Clare, it was thought that the essential nucleus of the conversations Clare had with her sisters should be transcribed and reorganized so that nothing of what she said would be lost. In other words, we do not intend to suggest a forgery, but rather to refer to the complex relationship that linked the written words to the reality that surrounded Clare and interacted with her. A hypothesis of this type does not do damage to the "essential" authenticity of the *Testament*.[49]

---

[47] PC III:32; Armstrong, *The Lady*, 162.

[48] Alessandra Bartolomei Romagnoli, "Il testamento di S. Chiara nella spiritualità femminile medioevale," in *Dialoghi con Chiara d' Assisi*. Atti delle Giornate di studio e riflessione per l'VIII Centenario di Santa Chiara, celebrato a S. Damiano di Assisi ottobre 1993-luglio 1994, ed. Luigi Giacometti (Santa Maria degli Angeli: Edizioni Porziuncola, 1995), 245.

[49] Romagnoli, "Il testamento di S. Chiara," 247.

As described above, Accrocca points to Leo as both scribe and author of the *Testament*, who took these written memories of Clare and framed them within a text that now responded to the struggle of the Poor Sisters after the death of Clare. In Brother Leo's time, the sisters were faced once again with another papal attempt to dislodge them from Clare's ideals. Leo inserted some things into these written memories, as suggested by Accrocca, that helped to address the new issues which the sisters had to face. As a faithful companion of Francis, Leo did a similar thing with his memories of Francis contained within the text of the *Assisi Compilation*. It is therefore not hard to imagine or believe that he would do the same for Clare, given that after the death of Francis, Brother Leo gravitated to Clare, who for him continued to be form and example of the Franciscan ideal.

But what Leo added was not simple invention. Clare and her sisters preserved the memory of Francis by preserving the writings which he had addressed to them. In this context Marco Bartoli's hypothesis of a Francis "Cycle of San Damiano" would provide a basis for the composite nature of Clare's *Testament*.[50] In his argument, Bartoli states that these major Franciscan sources are based on a common source: the story of Francis and the Cross of San Damiano and the prophecy concerning the Poor Ladies which he made while he was rebuilding that church which appears in the *Legend of the Three Companions*; Thomas of Celano's *Remembrance in the Desire of a Soul*; and Bonaventure's *Major Legend*. That common source, writes Bartoli, was also used as the basis for that memory of Francis's prophecy that appears in Clare's *Testament*. In addition, other writings of Francis addressed to Clare and the Poor Ladies, such as Francis's *Form of Life* and his *Last Will for the Poor Ladies*, which appear in chapter six of Clare's *Form of Life*, as well as his *Canticle of Exhortation for the Poor Ladies* – texts which are also suggested in Celano's *Remembrance* (#204) – are based on a written source preserved at San Damiano by Clare and her sisters. In addition, the story of the origin of Francis's *Canticle of Creatures* as told in the *Assisi Compilation* (#83, 85) would have been preserved at San Damiano where the text originated. He suggests that these written texts were placed in a narrative context by the sisters themselves at San Damiano,

---

[50] Marco Bartoli, "*Novitas clariana*. Chiara, testimone di Francesco," in *Chiara di Assisi*. Atti del XX Convegno internazionale, Assisi, 15-17 ottobre 1992. Società Internazionale di Studi Francescani Convegni, XX (Spoleto: CISAM, 1993), 157-85.

and served as the source for parallel stories that appeared in the later hagiographical tradition. He concluded by stating that it is certain

> that at San Damiano various writings of Francis were pre-served that later flowed into, in one way or another, the succes-sive compilations, and they certainly preserved the memories, probably orally, of all the episodes of the life of the saint, con-nected in some way to that place."[51]

Thus, Leo's role in the composition of Clare's *Testament* would be that of a true compiler of the memories of Clare and the sisters of Francis's role in the establishment of the life of the Poor Ladies, which he inserted into the written record of Clare's last words to her sisters. Leo did this to help the Poor Ladies themselves in a historical context of struggle to maintain the life and vision of Clare, their mother, and Francis, their Father.

III. INTERPRETING THE TEXT

Scholars have suggested various ways to approach the text from a structural point of view, each of which has merit.[52] Here I will follow the four-part structure suggested by Cesare Vaiani in his analysis of Clare's *Testament*.[53]

The first part of Clare's *Testament* (vv. 1-23) presents a reflection on the nature of the calling of Clare and her sisters' as the gift of a merciful, Trinitarian God. Citing a text from Paul, "Recognize your vocation" (1 Cor 1:26), Clare describes how this calling is a gift from the Father that is revealed in the Son of God. Francis taught the sisters in "word and example" (v. 5) how the Son of God became the "Way"

---

[51] Bartoli, *"Novitas clariana,"* 184.

[52] Lehmann summarizes a number of approaches in "La questione del testamento di s. Chiara," 298-305. In addition Edith van den Goorbergh proposes a chiastic struc-ture in her article, "Clare's Awareness of her Mission in the Church concerning Her Testament," *OFM Pro monialibus* 16 (1963): 18-19. An alternate structure is suggested by Clara Gennaro, *Chiara d'Assisi: Immagini di una donna* (Vicenza, Italy: L.I.E.F., 2000), 108-09.

[53] Cesare Vaiani, "Chiara nei suoi scritti," *Forma sororum* 36 (1999): 112-24; 215-28; 284-95. The entire article was published in ten parts from 1998-2001.

(John 14:6) for their form of life.[54] Inspired by the Holy Spirit (v. 11), Francis mediated this gift of God even before he himself had brothers. This reference is made in connection with Francis's prophecy, made while he was rebuilding San Damiano, that here one day women would come to glorify God by their way of life (*sancta conversatio*, v. 14). We spoke above of the question raised by the presence of this prophecy in the *Testament* given its almost identical form in the *Legend of the Three Companions*, but this reference serves here to underline the connection of Clare and her sisters with Francis from even before Clare's own conversion and her promise of obedience to Francis. Thus, Francis is presented as the agent of God's calling of Clare and her sisters from the beginning. The import of this event in the text, therefore, is that Francis was initiated in his role by God, and hence the connection with the brothers which derives from this cannot be severed.

Following this celebration of God's calling, mediated through Francis, that has been described as both "mercy" (v. 2), as "gift" (v. 6), and as "the abundant goodness of God" (v. 15), the text then turns to the obligation of the sisters to "return to him an increase of talents" (v. 18), a reference taken from the gospel of Matthew's parable of the talents (25:15-23). The way that the sisters are to return the gift to its source is by living as "example and mirror" (v. 19) for both those in the world as well as for each other. The image of the mirror is developed in Clare's letters to Agnes, but especially in the *Fourth Letter to Agnes* (vv. 14-24), where the mirror reflects the birth, life and passion of Jesus Christ. Here in the *Testament* this image of the mirror is developed to express the dynamic exchange and nature of the life of the Poor Ladies. The sisters "mirror" Christ to each other and to those outside the enclosure in the world. This "mirroring" is the "form" referred to above in the text, that is, the Son of God who "has become for us the

---

[54] Romagnoli, "Il testament di s. Chiara nella spiritualità femmile medioevale," 245-46, raises questions about the use made in the text of *vocatio* (vv. 4, 16), suggesting that it is used here in a technical sense of the call to a religious form of life, which did not originate until much later in history. However, the scriptural reference to 1 Corinthians points to the sense of the usage employed by Clare. Paul is speaking about how God chooses what is considered foolish by the world to shame the wise in the world, ultimately pointing to the wisdom of Cross as God's way of unmasking the values of the world. Here, in the context of conversion, the emphasis is not on a specifically religious vocation, but a Christian calling as the source for a way of being in the world. One can see this same usage of "calling" employed by Clare in 2LtAg 17, and by Francis in the CtExh 1.

Way" (v.5). In this sense, for Clare and her sisters, everything about their life is grace: both the origin of the life and the object of their life. While this form of life will be further described in terms of poverty and mutual love in the second and third sections of the text, this first section places everything about the life of the sisters in God.

There are two clear dynamics that the text has presented to this point. The first is the experienced conviction of Clare and her sisters that their form of life is the gift of the good God. The second dynamic is the obligation, deriving from this same gift of returning to God through a life of exemplarity, or in the words of the text, in being "mirror and example." The gift is given for living, and living the gift is the manner of returning what God has given. This is a perfect reflection of Francis' own understanding of the vocation of the Lesser Brothers as revealed by God.[55] For both the brothers and sisters, the form of life is the way of the gospel, that is, the example given in the birth, the life, and the death of Jesus Christ.

The second section of the *Testament* moves from this more theological reflection on the nature of the life of the Poor Ladies to a description of its historical origins, beginning with Clare's own conversion to a life of penance (vv. 24-36).[56] This section also begins by highlighting the role of Francis as the mediator of God's enlightenment leading Clare and her first sisters to conversion and the promise of obedience to Francis (vv. 24-25). Here again, the role of Francis in the life of the Poor Ladies is emphasized. The text states that Clare and her sisters promised Francis obedience (25-26), an action that had the effect of receiving Clare into the brotherhood. This is a striking statement because it clearly contradicts the prohibition of the *Earlier Rule* with

---

[55] See, for example, ER 17:17-19, which summarizes the life of the brothers described to that point as "returning" every good to God. Consult, Michael Blastic, "Prayer in the Writings of Francis and the Early Brothers," in *Franciscans at Prayer*, ed. Timothy J. Johnson (Leiden: Brill, 2007), 6-11.

[56] Here the parallel with the *Testament* of Francis becomes explicit, as Clare speaks about the Father enlightening "her heart to do penance" (TestCl 24), and Francis spoke about the Lord giving him, "Brother Francis, to do penance" (Test 1). Clare describes her life as a life of penance in her *Form of life* 6:1 in a strikingly similar manner: "After the Most High Heavenly Father saw fit by his grace to enlighten my heart to do penance according to the teaching and example of Saint Francis, shortly after his own conversion ..."

regard to receiving any woman into obedience.[57] The text goes on to describe how Francis observed the life of the sisters, and that as a result of what he saw – their deprivation, poverty, work, weakness and frailty, shame and contempt of the world[58] – he promised the same "loving care and special solicitude" (v. 29) as he had for his own brothers.[59] This reference precedes the actual arrival of the sisters at San Damiano, which itself is taken up in the following verses (30-36). In these verses, Clare affirms that it was Francis's will that Clare and the sisters came to San Damiano, after staying in other places only briefly (vv. 30-32). Once at San Damiano, Francis then wrote his *Form of Life* for the sisters according to the *Testament*. Then follows an affirmation that suggests Francis's continuing involvement with the Poor Ladies:

> While he was living he was not content to encourage us with many words and examples to the love of holy poverty and its observance, but he gave us many writings (*plura scripta*) that, after his death, we would in no way turn away from it, as the Son of God never wished to turn away from this holy poverty while he lived in the world (vv. 34-35).[60]

---

[57] ER 12:4, "Absolutely no woman may be received to obedience by any brother, but after spiritual advice has been given to her, let her do penance wherever she wants." This negative statement was an addition to the text made sometime after their initial approval by Innocent III in 1209, surely after Lateran IV in 1215. That Clare should reaffirm this promise of obedience at the end of her life, thus contradicting the *Earlier Rule* of the brothers, a text she used in the composition of her own *Forma vitae*, reflects her struggle to maintain this connection with the brothers after Francis's death. See the comments of Jacques Dalarun, *Francis of Assisi and the Feminine* (St. Bonaventure, NY: Franciscan Institute Publications, 2006), 45-54 [the original Italian edition appeared in Rome: Viella, 1994].

[58] Here Clare employs some of the same adjectives that she uses to describe Jesus Christ in the mirror of the Cross in her *Fourth Letter to Agnes*, vv. 19-23.

[59] These verses of the *Testament* summarize the *Form of Life* that Francis wrote for Clare and the Poor Ladies early on in their existence. The text of Francis's *Form of Life* is preserved only in Clare's *Form of Life* 6:3-4, and here verse four is echoed in the text of the *Testament*.

[60] As the Poor Clares themselves have demonstrated with regard to their *Form of Life*, Clare and her sisters had copies of the *Earlier Rule*, the *Later Rule*, the *Testament*, as well as other texts that connected Francis to San Damiano. See Federazione s. Chiara di Assisi delle Clarisse di Umbria-Sardegna, *Chiara di Assisi e le sue fonti legislative: Sinossi cromatica* (Padua: Edizioni Messaggero, 2003).

These "many writings" provided the concrete evidence for what Clare was attempting to establish in her *Testament*, that is, the integral connection with the brothers in sharing a form of life given by God, and the centrality of poverty to the integrity of that form of life. The connection with the brothers is highlighted in Francis's *Form of Life* for the sisters, and the integrity of poverty is underlined in Francis's *Last Will* for Clare and her sisters, also preserved in her own *Form of Life* (VI:7-9). These writings of Francis preserve the memory of the origins of the way of life of the Poor Ladies and in recounting this memory, Clare is at the same time calling her sisters to preserve this life into and for the future.

The third section of the *Testament* (vv. 37-55) underlines the centrality of poverty to the form of the life of the Poor Ladies. In connection to poverty, Francis is recognized as the pillar and support for the sisters and the "only consolation after God" (v. 39). One can read in these words the real struggle of Clare and the sisters to remain faithful to "Lady Poverty" and to "never in any way turn away from her." This is the real history lived by Clare and her sisters, who resisted many attempts by the papacy and papal curia to convince Clare to receive possessions. The anguish palpable in these words also reflects the contrasting history of the Lesser Brothers, who, beginning in 1230 with Gregory IX's *Quo elongati*, sought modifications of the vow of poverty. This left Clare virtually alone in the struggle to preserve the charism of her founder and friend, Francis. It is in this context that the *Testament* refers to Clare's struggle to have "most holy poverty" protected by "privileges" (v. 42) from Innocent and his successors. This is the text on which Maleczek hinged his argument against the authenticity of Clare's *Testament*. However, in this section, Clare does not make any reference to a written document, and even though she does use the term "privileges," it is unclear exactly what was intended.[61]

Clare then commends all her sisters, "both those present and those to come" (v.44), to the Church, specifically to the Cardinal Protector of the Lesser Brothers, so that they would never turn away from poverty. Clare invokes the love of the God, "who was placed poor in the crib, lived poor in the world, and remained naked on the cross" (v.45),

---

[61] See above the discussion in Part I of this essay. Also see Emore Paoli, "Introduzione" to Clare's *Opuscula* in *Fontes Franciscani*, 2240-42, and Michael Cusato's article referenced above in footnote 29.

as the motive for the Cardinal Protector's oversight and encourage-
ment of the sisters' following of "the poverty and humility of his most
Beloved Son and his glorious Mother" (v.46).[62] This request of the
Pope and Cardinal reflects the ecclesial consciousness of Clare and her
sisters, and underlines how the sisters make present in the church the
reality of the humble and poor Son of God and his mother.

In this section, there is a clear affirmation of the ecclesial significance of the life of the Poor Ladies. The poverty that Clare and her
sisters live is important not only for themselves, but also for the church
at large in that they are mirrors and examples of the Son of God. Poverty is thus not conceived of merely as a virtue or an ascetical practice,
but rather as an encounter with the person of Jesus Christ, made available to others in the mirror of San Damiano.

After commending the sisters to the church, the text then turns
to the Lesser Brothers, recalling again Francis's role in the origin and
development of the Poor Ladies. Clare entrusts her sisters, present and
future, to the successors of Francis "and to the entire religion" that
they help the sisters "above all in better observing most holy poverty"
(v. 51). The reference to the "entire religion" of the Lesser Brothers
is truly striking, as Clare places this obligation not only in the hands
of the leadership of the Order, but also of each of the brothers. Here
Clare uses the image of a plant to describe the relation between the sisters and Francis as one of care. This is exactly what Francis promised
in his *Form of Life* for Clare and the Poor Ladies. So, in effect, Clare
is simply asking the brothers to honor the commitment that Francis
made to them at the beginning.

Verse fifty-two addresses the possibility of the sisters leaving San
Damiano and going elsewhere. While this does seem to be out of place
in the last years of Clare's life, it does fit with the events following
Clare's death. Within four years of her death, the sisters moved up
to the city of Assisi and took up residence near the place where Clare
was buried, the church of San Giorgio. The Basilica of St. Clare was
begun in 1257, together with the monastery of the Poor Ladies. After
1264, there were many attempts to impose on these sisters the *Rule of
Urban IV* that created the "Order of Saint Clare." The sisters themselves requested of Clement IV the continued opportunity to observe

---

[62] Here again one can see the parallel and the significance of what Clare has to say
to Agnes in her *Fourth Letter*, vv. 24-24.

Clare's *Form of Life*, which he granted with the bull *Solet annuere* on December 31, 1266. This bull confirmed their observance of the Rule of Clare, originally approved by Innocent IV in 1253, and thus placed these sisters outside the Order of Saint Clare established by Urban IV. However, prior to this bull, and subsequent to Clare's death, great pressure was placed on her sisters to adopt a form of life with a different spirit. This is the situation that verse fifty-two addresses, by saying that if at any time the sisters leave San Damiano and go to another place, "let them be bound, wherever they may be after my death, to observe that form of poverty that we have promised God and our most blessed father Francis."

In the conclusion of this section of the *Testament* focused on the observance of poverty, Clare specifies that her successors must not acquire more land that is necessary for the "integrity and privacy" of the monastery" (v. 53-54). Here again she echoes the prescription in the *Form of Life*.[63] This is the clearest description of the nature of poverty with regard to ownership lived by Clare and her sisters at San Damiano, a poverty which clearly distinguishes them from other monastic foundations. It was this radical form of poverty that placed the sisters in a relationship of dependence on God, the author of their life, and on the Lesser Brothers, who provided for both their spiritual and material needs.

The final section of the *Testament* (vv. 56-79) deals with the common life of the sisters in terms of mutual charity.[64] It begins with an exhortation to remain faithful to the "way of holy simplicity, humility and poverty and also the integrity of our holy way of living" (v. 56). This exhortation is a return to the theme of the purpose or end of the life of the sisters; that is, exemplarity. Living in this manner, the sisters "spread the fragrance of a good reputation" (v. 58). However, the text immediately underlines the fact that this reputation is not solely the work of the sisters, but the "largesse" of the Father's mercy and grace.

---

[63] *Form of Life* 6:12: "[T]hat is, by not receiving or having possessions or ownership either of themselves or through an intermediary, or even anything that might reasonably be called ownership, except as much land as necessity requires for the integrity and proper seclusion of the monastery, and the land may not be cultivated except as a garden for the needs of the sisters."

[64] Clara Gennaro, *Chiara di Assisi: Immagini di una donna*, 118-19, describes this mutual love as a "visible expression, sacrament, of that which the sisters carry within themselves ..."

This mercy of the Father, this interior gift of grace, needs to become manifest in deeds. Mutual charity is the way of growth in the love of God and one another (v. 60).[65] Thus, the sisters are called to put into practice the great commandment of love of God and love of neighbor.

The text then turns to the role of the Abbess and the other sisters. First, "that sister who will be in the office of the sisters" must lead by example, so that the sisters might obey out of love rather than because of her office (vv. 61-62). This sister must provide for her sisters like a mother, each according to need (vv. 63-64). The statement has the clear implication that this role demands a personal relationship, based on the specific needs of each sister – holy unity does not imply uniformity, even with regard to the distribution of alms! In addition, this sister must be "so kind and affable" (v. 65) that she is approachable and worthy of the confidence of the sisters.[66] In turn, the sisters who are subject to the Abbess must remember that "they have given up their wills" (v.67). The "charity, humility and unity" (v.69) that characterizes the relationships of the sisters then becomes a help to the Abbess in her burden of office, and changes "what is painful and bitter" into "sweetness" (v. 70). This reflects the experience of Francis in his own conversion,[67] and points to that dimension of the life of penance with regard to the real experience of human relationships.

Following this description of the Abbess' role is the exhortation to persevere in this "straight" way in order to enter through "narrow" gate which opens into life (v. 71). The images are dynamic, and un-

---

[65] This is a reflection of what the brothers articulate in the *Earlier Rule* 9:5-6, "Let them love one another, as the Lord says: This is my commandment: love one another as I have loved you. Let them express the love they have for one another by their deeds, as the Apostle says: Let us not love in word or speech, but in deed and truth." Felice Accrocca, "Verso il Getsemani? Chiara, la comunità delle sorelle e la vita quotidiana a San Damiano," *Analecta T.O.R.* 26 (1995): 72-88, reflects on the real difficulties Clare and her sisters experienced within the monastery.

[66] This section of the *Testament* reflects the description of the relationship between the Abbess and the other sisters in the *Form of Life* 8:12-16, and 10:1-7, both of which texts emphasize the unity of mutual love that should characterize all the sisters.

[67] Francis's *Testament* 3. Clara Gennaro, *Chiara di Assisi: Immagini di una donna*, 120, comments that from the usage of this image from Francis's *Testament*, "we can deduce how the refusal of Clare to take the office of Abbess was not that of a taken for granted humility, and in addition how the task of presiding was not without bitterness and difficulty."

derline the fact that the choice to follow this way is not made once for all, but must be regularly renewed and re-chosen. The text underlines the real challenge of following this way of poverty and charity, but promises blessings to those who persevere (v.73). To turn away from this way is to "do a great wrong" to Jesus and his mother, to Francis, and to the church, and those who do are cursed. This leads Clare to pray to Jesus, to Mary, and to Francis that God might give them final perseverance (v. 78). Again, the text emphasizes Clare's awareness that not only the vocation, but also the journey, is a grace and depends on the goodness of God.

The *Testament* concludes with the affirmation that the purpose of "this writing" is to help better observe the way described, that is, the *Form of Life* approved by the church, and promised by the sisters. The *Testament* is a "sign of the blessing of the Lord and our most blessed father Francis, and of my blessing, your mother and handmaid" (v. 79).[68]

The *Testament* breathes with a sense of preoccupation, and is written in that manner so as to preserve the form of life lived at San Damiano by Clare and her sisters in a moment of challenge. The emphasis on Francis as the mediator of this way of life, and as the continual support and foundation of those undertaking it, together with the reaffirmation of poverty as the heart of this way are the means the text uses to preserve both poverty and the connection with the Lesser Brothers. Drawing on the historical memory and texts left by Francis to the sisters, the *Testament* reminds the sisters of what is at stake for their future. For this reason, Clare's *Testament* has been read by the Poor Ladies throughout their history. It is a precious document, a witness to the real circumstances accompanying Clare and her sisters while she lived, and an admonition to her followers after her death, involved in maintaining the "gift" given to them by the Father of mercies, through the agency of Francis. It calls forth from the sisters their total reliance on the mercy of God, the source of their vocation. One can see in this regard how useful and important the text of Clare's *Testament* would become to the Poor Clares throughout the centuries, as well as to the Lesser Brothers.[69]

---

[68] This statement parallels that of Francis in his *Testament* 34.

[69] See for example, Brufani, "La Memoria di Chiara d'Assisi," in *Clara claris praeclara*, 501-23.

IV. BIBLIOGRAPHY

Manuscripts and Editions

Bartoli Langeli, Attilio. *Gli autografi di frate Francesco e di frate Leone.* Corpus Christianorum, Autographa Medii Aevi V. Brussels: Brepols, 2000. 104-30 with tables.

Boccali, Giovanni. "Testamento e benedizione di s. Chiara. Nuovo codice latino." *Archivum Franciscanum Historicum* 82 (1989): 273-305.

Claire d'Assisi Écrits. Marie-France Becker, Jean-François Godet and Thaddée Matura, eds. Sources Chrétiennes 32. Paris: Les Éditions du Cerf, 1985. 21-27.

Ciccarelli, Diego. "Contributi alla recesione degli scritti di s. Chiara." *Miscellanea Francescana* 79 (1979): 347-74.

Studies

Accrocca, Felice. "Chiara e l'ordine Francescano." In *Clara Claris Praeclara.* 339-79.

Chiara d'Assisi: La Regola, le lettere, e il testamento spirituale. Tutti gli scritti della santa di Assisi. Intro. Felice Accrocca. Trans. Modestino Cerra. Casale Monferrato: Edizioni Piemme, 2004.

Clara Claris Praeclara. Atti del Convegno Internazionale. L'esperienza cristiana e la memoria di Chiara d'Assisi in occasione del 750° anniversario della morte. Assisi 20-22 novembre 2003. Santa Maria degli Angeli: Edizioni Porziuncola, 2004.

Cremaschi, Giovanna and Agnese Acquadro. *Scritti di santa Chiara d'Assisi.* Commento Vol. I. Santa Maria degli Angeli: Edizioni Porziuncola, 1994.

Gennaro, Clara. *Chiara d'Assisi: Immagini di una donna.* Vicenza, Italy: L.I.E.F., 2000.

Lainati, Chiara Augusta. "Testamento di santa Chiara." *Dizionario Francescano: Spiritualità.* Second edition. Ed. Ernesto Caroli. Padua: Edizioni Messaggero Padova, 1995. Cols. 2045-2064.

Lehmann, Leonhard. "La questione del testamento di s. Chiara." In *Clara Claris Praeclara.* 257-305.

Lopez, Sebastián. "Lectura teológica del Testamento de santa Clara." *Selecciones de Franciscanismo* 11 (1982): 299-312.

Romagnoli, Alessandra Bartolomei. "Il testamento di s. Chiara nella spiritualità femminile medioevale." In *Dialoghi con Chiara di Assisi.* Ed. Luigi Giacometti. Santa Maria degli Angeli: Edizioni Porziuncola, 1995. 241-59.

Van den Goorbergh, Edith. "Clare's Awareness of Her Mission in the Church Concerning Her Testament." *OFM Pro monialibus* 16 (1993): 15-26.

Vaiani, Cesare. "Chiara nei suoi scritti." *Forma sororum* 35 (1998): 82-102; 36 (1999): 112-24, 215-28, 284-95; 37 (2000): 49-55, 87-93, 176-81, 257-69, 319-29; 38 (2001): 45-54.

CLARE'S BLESSING

JEAN-FRANÇOIS GODET-CALOGERAS

INTRODUCTION

At the end of her *Testament*, Clare announced a blessing for all her sisters:

> So that it would be better observed, I am leaving you, my dearest and beloved sisters, present and to come, this writing as a sign of the blessing of the Lord and of our most blessed father Francis, and of my blessing, your mother and servant.[1]

The *Legenda sanctae Clarae* confirms that Clare called down "a large grace of blessing upon all the ladies of the poor monasteries, those present as well as those future."[2]

Since the Middle Ages, different manuscripts have carried a blessing of Clare in various languages and to various beneficiaries. The oldest blessing is a copy in Middle High German, and is addressed to Agnes of Prague. A second blessing is in Latin and addressed to Ermentrude of Bruges. Finally, a third blessing, in Latin as well as in Middle French, Middle Italian, and Middle Dutch, is addressed to all the sisters. All of these versions offer in substance the same content, whether the addressee is individual or collective.

---

[1] TestCl 79: *Hoc scriptum, ut melius debeat observari, relinquo vobis carissimis et dilectis sororibus meis praesentibus et venturis, in signum benedictionis Domini et beatissimi patris nostri Francisci et benedictionis meae, matris et ancillae vestrae.*

[2] LCl 45: ... *omnibus dominabus monasteriorum pauperum tam praesentibus quam futuris largam benedictionem gratiam imprecatur.*

Thus, there is a tradition attesting that Clare composed a blessing, if not several blessings. Although it is conceivable that Clare sent a blessing to various addressees, it is dubious that she would have written in a variety of languages. The study of the manuscript tradition should clarify the situation.

I. ESTABLISHING THE TEXT

The blessing addressed to Agnes of Prague is only present in Middle High German manuscripts, where it follows the four letters of Clare to Agnes. The oldest of those manuscripts is dated 1350.[3] However, the manuscript of Milan[4] that contains a Latin copy of the *Letters to Agnes of Prague* does not have the text of the blessing. Moreover, the German text seems to have taken the Latin text of the blessing, addressed to Ermentrude of Bruges, as a model. Hence its authenticity is more than dubious and is not accepted by the recent scholarship. The blessing sent to Ermentrude of Bruges is a Latin text copied in 1679 by Sebastian Bouvier, a friar minor from the Flemish province.[5] This text does not appear anywhere else, not even in the *Annales Minorum* of Luke Wadding or the *Acta Sanctorum* of the Bollandists. Hence its authenticity is also very unlikely. Although those two personal blessings are most probably apocryphal, we reproduce here their texts for information purpose.

The blessing to all the sisters has a much larger and more authentic manuscript tradition, both in vernacular and in Latin. The oldest text in vernacular is written in Middle French and is found in a manuscript from the end of the fifteenth century.[6] The first part of that manuscript

---

[3] Walter Seton, "Some New Sources for the Life of Blessed Agnes of Bohemia, including some Chronological Notes and a New Text of the Benediction of Saint Clare," *Archivum Franciscanum Historicum* 7 (1914): 185-97, and "The Oldest Text of the Benediction of Saint Clare of Assisi," *Revue d'Histoire Franciscaine* 2 (1925): 88-90; Mark Borkowski, "A Second Middle High German Translation of the Benediction of Saint Clare," *Franciscan Studies* 36 (1976): 90-104.

[4] Milan, Biblioteca Capitolare di Sant'Ambrogio, M-10, ff. 50v-57v.

[5] David de Kok, "De origine Ordinis S. Clarae in Flandria," *Archivum Franciscanum Historicum* 7 (1914): 244-45.

[6] Ubald d'Alençon, "Le plus ancien texte de la Bénédiction, du Privilège de Pauvreté et du Testament de Sainte Claire d'Assise," *Revue d'Histoire Franciscaine* 1 (1924): 469-82 (472-73).

contains Clare's *Blessing* (folios 19r-20r), the *Privilege of Poverty* of Innocent III (folios 20r-22r), and Clare's *Testament* (folios 22r-30v). A version in Middle Italian is found in two manuscripts of the Poor Clare monastery of Urbino in the Marches.[7] Both manuscripts were written in the fifteenth century and offer the text of the *Blessing* after the text of Clare's *Testament*. A shorter version of Clare's *Blessing* in Middle Italian is also found in the *Chronicle* of Mark of Lisbon.[8] Those Middle French and Middle Italian versions of the *Blessing* are also reproduced in the *Seraphicae Legislationis Textus Originales*.[9] Finally, there are nine manuscripts of Clare's *Blessing* in Middle Dutch,[10] the oldest of which was written in 1460.

More important than these are four Latin manuscripts of a blessing of Clare for all the sisters. One copy is in the Poor Clare monastery of Montevergine in Messina, Sicily;[11] another is the codex 1258 of the Archivo Histórico Nacional in Madrid;[12] a third one is the codex C 63 of the Library of the University of Uppsala in Sweden;[13] and a fourth copy is in the codex II.1561 of the Royal Library in Brussels, Belgium.[14] Most of those manuscripts are from the fourteenth and fifteenth centuries and have a very similar text of the *Blessing* following Clare's *Testament*. Of particular interest is the manuscript of Messina: an extremely small manuscript (mm. 75 x 50), of 34 folios, that contains only Clarian texts: Clare's *Form of Life* (ff. 3r-20v), the epilogue of the approbation by Cardinal Rainaldo and Pope Innocent IV (ff. 20v-21r), the *Privilege of Poverty* of Innocent III (ff. 21r-23r), the bull *Solet an-*

---

[7] Diego Ciccarelli, "Contributi alla recensione degli Scritti di S. Chiara," *Miscellanea Francescana* 79 (1979): 347-74 (353-55).

[8] Mark of Lisbon, *Cronache*, vol. I (Venice, 1582), book 8, chapter 34, 240.

[9] *Seraphicae Legislationis Textus Originales* (Quaracchi: Collegium S. Bonaventurae, 1897), 281-82.

[10] David de Kok, "S. Clarae Benedictionis Textus Neerlandici," *Archivum Franciscanum Historicum* 27 (1934): 387-98.

[11] Zeffirino Lazzeri, "La *forma vitae* di S. Chiara ... a Messina?" *Chiara d'Assisi: Rassegna del Protomonastero* 2 (1954): 137-41; Diego Ciccarelli, "I manoscritti francescani della Biblioteca Universitaria di Messina," *Miscellanea Francescana* 78 (1978): 517-23, and "Contributi alla recensione degli scritti di S. Chiara," 349-51.

[12] Angel Uribe, "Nuevos escritos ineditos villacrecianos," *Archivo Ibero-Americano* 34 (1974): 303-34.

[13] Margarete Andersen-Schmitt, *Manuscripta Mediaevalia Upsaliensia* (Uppsala: Almqvist & Wiksell, 1970), 89.

[14] Giovanni Boccali, "Testamento e benedizione di S. Chiara: Nuovo codice latino," *Archivum Franciscanum Historicum* 82 (1989): 277.

nuere of Innocent IV of August 9, 1253 (ff. 23r-24v), Clare's *Testament* (ff. 25r-32r), and Clare's *Blessing* to all the sisters (ff. 32v-33v). It came to Messina with Saint Eustochia Calafato (1434-1485),[15] who brought it with her when she left the monastery of Monteluce[16] in Perugia to found the monastery of Montevergine in 1464. From careful examination, scholars have agreed that this is the best manuscript for the text of both Clare's *Blessing* as well as her *Testament*.[17]

In the past decades, given the established manuscript tradition, and given the clear link to Clare's *Testament*, the *Blessing* to all the sisters has usually been considered as authentic.[18] This was until 1995, when Werner Maleczek raised serious questions regarding the authenticity of the *Privilege of Poverty* of Innocent III and Clare's *Testament*.[19] Maleczek, first of all, quite convincingly demonstrated that the *Privilege of Poverty* of Innocent III was a forgery based on the authentic document granted by Gregory IX in 1228. Then, because there is in Clare's *Testament* an explicit reference to a *Privilege of Poverty* granted by Innocent III, Maleczek questioned the authenticity of that *Testament*. Both documents are linked in the manuscript tradition, in the same way that the *Blessing* is linked to the *Testament*. Maleczek focused on the Messina manuscript as the source of the whole tradition that he considered

---

[15] Ciccarelli, "I manoscritti francescani," 517-521; Francesco Terrizzi, "Documenti relativi alla Vita della beata Eustochia Calafato," *Archivum Franciscanum Historicum* 58 (1965): 280-329; Fausta Casolini, *Santa Eustochia Calafato* (Messina: n.p., 1988).

[16] Ugolino Nicolini, "I Minori Osservanti di Monteripido e lo *scriptorium* delle clarisse di Monteluce in Perugia nei secoli XV e XVI," *Picenum Seraphicum* 8 (1971): 100-30.

[17] Mainly Diego Ciccarelli, "Contributi alla Recensione degli Scritti di S. Chiara," *Miscellanea Francescana* 79 (1979): 347-74; Jean-François Godet, in *Claire d'Assise: Écrits* (Paris: Éditions du Cerf, 1985), 27-28; Giovanni Boccali, "Testamento e benedizione di S. Chiara," *Archivum Franciscanum Historicum* 82 (1989): 273-305.

[18] Engelbert Grau, "Die Schriften der heiligen Klara und die Werke ihrer Biographen," in *Movimento religioso femminile e francescanesimo nel secolo XIII* (Assisi: S.I.S.F., 1980), 193-238: "Von der Form und vom Inhalt her sind ... keinerlei Einwände gegen die Echtheit des Segens der hl. Klara zu erheben. Stil und Ausdrucksweise der Briefe, des Testamentes und des Segens erweisen sich als einheitlich" (221-22). (From the form and from the contents ... there can be absolutely no objection to the authenticity of the blessing of saint Clare. The style and the expressions of the letters, the testament and the blessing prove themselves homogeneous).

[19] Werner Maleczek, "Das *Privilegium Paupertatis* Innocenz' III. und das Testament der Klara von Assisi: Überlegungen zur Frage ihrer Echtheit," *Collectanea Franciscana* 65 (1995): 5-82.

apocryphal. Given the link between the manuscript and Eustochia Calafato, Maleczek argued that it had been written in Umbria, most likely in the *scriptorium* of the Poor Clares of Monteluce in Perugia, in the middle of the fifteenth century, at the time of the Observant Reform in central Italy, to defend a radical position on poverty. Maleczek concluded that Clare's *Testament* was a forgery like the *Privilege of Poverty* of Innocent III. Such a conclusion, of course, also brought a verdict of inauthenticity to Clare's *Blessing*.

Maleczek's work generated a storm in the world of Clarian studies. Responses followed soon after: in an extensive article published the following year,[20] Niklaus Kuster countered Maleczek's arguments, as did Emore Paoli in his introduction to the writings of Clare for *Fontes Franciscani*.[21] The result was a stalemate: for one side all is forgery, for the other all is authentic. For Maleczek, the *Privilege of Poverty* of Innocent III and Clare's *Testament* – and consequently also Clare's *Blessing* – are linked in an operation of forgery that happened in Umbria in the middle of the fifteenth century, and of which the Messina manuscript is the written evidence. For Kuster, such an argument is unacceptable, as those texts belong to the story of San Damiano in the thirteenth century.

At last, a magistral work of Attilio Bartoli Langeli in 2000 brought new light to the question.[22] After studying the autographs of Brother Francis, Bartoli Langeli turned his attention to the autographs of Brother Leo written in red ink on the famous *Chartula* with the *Praises of God* and a *Blessing*. He examined Leo's handwriting as it appears on the *Chartula* and also in the so-called *Breviary of Saint Francis*, and then compared the handwriting to the one in the Messina manuscript. Already in 1954, Zeffirino Lazzeri had suggested that the Messina manuscript not only had come from Umbria, but had probably been written by somebody close to Clare, maybe Brother Leo.[23] Almost half a century later, after a careful and meticulous examination of the text

---

[20] Niklaus Kuster, "Das Armutsprivileg Innocenz' III. und Klaras Testament: Echt oder Raffinierte Fälschungen?" *Collectanea Franciscana* 66 (1996): 5-95.

[21] Emore Paoli, "Introduzione," in *Fontes Franciscani*, ed. Enrico Menestò and Stefano Brufani (Assisi: Edizioni Porziuncola, 1995), 2237-51.

[22] Attilio Bartoli Langeli, *Gli Autografi di Frate Francesco e di Frate Leone* (Turnhout: Brepols, 2000).

[23] Lazzeri, "La *forma vitae* di S. Chiara," 138-41.

and the handwriting in the Messina manuscript,[24] Bartoli Langeli gave his own conclusion: "It is my opinion that the Messina manuscript was written by the hand of Brother Leo."[25]

If the Messina manuscript was written by Leo – and, almost a decade later, nobody has contradicted Bartoli Langeli or proved him wrong – the question of the authenticity of Clare's *Testament* and *Blessing* takes another turn. What is certain, and maybe should suffice, is that Leo was very close to Clare as he was to Francis. Was he not by Clare's bed when she was dying, as the *Legenda sanctae Clarae* tells us?[26] It seems, therefore, that we are caught in a sort of triangle of San Damiano.

II. APPROACHING THE TEXT

The sources of Clare's *Blessing* are predominantly biblical. From the Old Testament, there is only one obvious borrowing: in verses 2-4, the text of the Aaronic blessing in the book of Numbers.[27] Francis had already used this in the *Chartula* he gave to Brother Leo.[28] The expression "in heaven and on earth" that appears in verses 8 and 12 may be reminiscent of a blessing found in the book of Genesis.[29] But Clare's *Blessing* borrows much more from the New Testament: the gospels of Matthew, Luke, and John, and Paul's letters to the Corinthians and the Thessalonians.

The *Blessing* begins with the traditional invocation of the Trinity, borrowed from the gospel of Matthew, when Jesus gives his last instructions to his disciples.[30] The mention of perseverance until the end in verse 5 is reminiscent of Jesus' mission teachings to his disciples.[31]

---

[24] Bartoli Langeli, *Gli Autografi*, 108-24.

[25] Bartoli Langeli, *Gli Autografi*, 125: "La mia opinione è che il manoscritto messinese sia della mano di frate Leone."

[26] LCl 45: *Adstant illi duo beati Francisci socii benedicti, quorum unus Angelus moerens ipse, solatur moerentes; alter Leo, recedentis lectulum osculatur* ("Are present those two blessed companions of blessed Francis; one, Angelo, mourning himself, consoles those who are mourning; the other, Leo, kisses the bed of the one who is departing").

[27] Num 6:24-26.

[28] BlL 1-2.

[29] Gen 27:28.

[30] Matt 28:19.

[31] Matt 10:22.

The expression "heavenly Father" of verse 8, although quite traditional, is reminiscent of several passages of the gospel of Matthew.[32] The
expression "Father of mercies" is borrowed from Paul's second letter
to the Corinthians.[33] The final verse of the *Blessing* is reminiscent of
several passages of the New Testament.[34]

Clare's *Blessing* offers several similarities with other early Franciscan writings as well. We have already mentioned Francis's *Chartula*.
Other similarities with Francis's writings include the *Earlier Rule*,[35] the
Letter to the Faithful,[36] the *Letter to the Order*,[37] the *Letter to a Minister*,[38]
and the *Testament*.[39] Passages of Clare's *Blessing* also have similarities
with Clare's *Form of Life*[40] and Clare's *Testament*,[41] which reinforces the
argument in favor of the authenticity.

We have already seen how the manuscript tradition clearly links
Clare's *Blessing* to the end of her *Testament*. The texts themselves are
obviously very close to one another: the *Blessing* seems to prolong and
conclude the *Testament*. The nature of both documents tells that they
must originate in the last times of Clare's life on earth. This seems to
be confirmed by verse 11 of the *Blessing*: "I bless you in my life and
after my death."

III. Interpreting the Text

Clare's *Blessing* begins with the invocation of the Trinity, which is
also commonly called the sign of the cross: what follows is given "in
the name of the Father, the Son and the Holy Spirit." While this is a
declaration of Christian faith, it is also a call on the power of God: *No-
men est omen* ("the name is everything").

---

[32] Matt 6:14, 6:26, 15:13, 18:35.
[33] 2 Cor 1:3.
[34] Luke 1:28, Matt 28:20, 2 Cor 13:11-13.
[35] ER Prologue 1 and BlCl 1.
[36] 2LtF 86 and BlCl 1.
[37] LOrd 1 and BlCl 1; LOrd 49 and BlCl 16.
[38] LMin 1 and BlCl 2.
[39] Test 40 and BlCl 8, 12.
[40] FLCl 1:3, 6:1 and BlCl 6.
[41] TestCl 5, 17, 24, 30, 36-37, 46-48, 50, 52, 57, 77, 79 and BlCl 6; TestCl 7, 17,
75, 77 and BlCl 7; TestCl 75 and BlCl 10; TestCl 2, 58 and BlCl 12.

Verses 2 to 5 follow the very blessing that Clare, like Francis, borrows from the book of Numbers. As Francis added to the number of those to whom he was addressing his blessing, Clare adds her personal touch by naming those to whom she is addressing her blessing.

A third part (verses 6-10) is a prayer of true intercession. Clare implores the blessing of the heavenly Father through the intercession of Francis and all saints, of Michael and all angels, of the Blessed Mother Mary, and through the mercy of Jesus Christ. She then (verses 11-13) blesses her sisters: "I bless you ..." and punctuates her personal blessing with an amen.

And yet the blessing is not over. Clare is compelled to add a fifth and final part, a conclusion in form of summary of her recommendations to her sisters (verses 14-16), followed by a final amen.

Clare's *Blessing* is a relatively long text – at least for a blessing – well articulated and with a rich vocabulary. A first image is the image of God's face, a face of mercy that brings peace. The importance of mercy in the life and writings of the early Franciscans is well known and can be summarized in the first lines of Francis's *Testament*.[42] For Clare as well, God is *misercordia*, mercy, and she borrows the expression from Paul's letter: *Pater misericordiarum*, Father of mercies. The Lord Jesus Christ, too, has mercy; mercy is definitely God's mark.

Clare uses another interesting image about the blessed Virgin Mary. She does not call her *mater*, mother, but *genitrix*, the one who bore Jesus and gave birth to him. *Genitrix* is a word that Francis also used in his *Salutation of the Blessed Virgin Mary*: "Hail, Lady, holy Queen, holy Mary who has born God."[43] It is also a word that in the whole Bible is only found in the *Song of Songs*,[44] from which Clare borrows in her last letter to Agnes of Prague, to evoke that which she longs for as she approaches death.[45]

---

[42] Test 1-3: *Dominus ita dedit michi fratri Francisci incipere faciendi penitentiam. Quia cum essem in peccatis nimis michi videbatur amarum videre leprosos. Et ipse Dominus conduxit me inter illos et feci misericordiam cum illis. Et recedente me ab ipsis, id quod videbatur michi amarum, conversum fuit michi in dulcedinem animi et corporis* ("The Lord gave me, brother Francis, to begin to do penance like this. For, when I was in sin, it seemed to me extremely bitter to see lepers. And the Lord himself led me among them, and I did mercy with them. And while I was departing from them, what seemed bitter to me had been converted into sweetness of the spirit and of the body").

[43] SalBVM 1: *Ave Domina, sancta Regina, sancta Dei genitrix Maria.*

[44] Song 3:4, 6:8 and 8:5.

[45] 4LAg 30-34.

In presenting herself, Clare employs the same words she has used in her *Letters*, in her *Form of Life* and in her *Testament*; she is the *ancilla*, the maidservant;[46] she is the *plantula*, the little plant, that is, the foundation of Francis;[47] and, even though she professes her unworthiness, she is the sister and the mother of the Poor Sisters, present and to come.[48]

From both her *Testament* and the *Legenda sanctae Clarae*,[49] it is clear that Clare wanted to bless her sisters before her death. The Bible and medieval hagiography contain numerous blessings by dying founders and foundresses. However, Clare introduces something original.

First, she uses the Aaronic blessing. Indeed, in doing so, she probably copies Francis, because in the Middle Ages, that blessing was reserved to priests and deacons. However, this obviously did not deter Clare from using it, which shows again her freedom and her assertiveness on the spiritual level.

While Clare blesses her sisters, it seems also that she did not have only them in mind. When she writes "and a spiritual father and a spiritual mother also have blessed and will bless their spiritual sons and daughters,"[50] who is the spiritual father if not Francis, and the spiritual mother if not herself? Then, the spiritual sons and daughters are no other than the brothers and the sisters of the Franciscan movement.

In her *Blessing*, Clare goes also beyond the limits of time and space. She does not pray only for the sisters living at her time in San Damiano, but also for all the Poor Sisters, everywhere and whenever they are and will be.[51] And she builds a bridge between heaven and earth, between the Church Militant and the Church Triumphant.[52]

---

[46] See 1LAg 2, 2LAg 2, 3LAg 2, 4LAg 2, FLCl 1:3 and 10:4-5, TestCl 37.

[47] See FLCl 1:3, TestCl 37, 79. On the meaning of *plantula* as religious foundation in the Middle Ages, see Albert Blaise, *Lexicon Latinitatis Medii Aevi* (Turnhout: Brepols, 1975), 694: *plantula*.

[48] See 4LAg 5, 33, 37, FLCl 1:5 and 4:7, TestCl 63, 68-69, 79.

[49] TestCl 79; LCl 45.

[50] BCl 13: *et pater et mater spiritualis filiis et filiabus suis spiritualibus et benedixit et benedicet*.

[51] BCl 7.

[52] BCl 8-12.

To end her *Blessing*, Clare summarizes wonderfully what living the Gospel has meant for her and Francis: love God, yourself and your sisters.[53] That was at the core of Francis's message:

> But how blessed and blessed are those who cherish God and do as the Lord himself says in the Gospel: You will cherish the Lord your God with all your heart and all your mind, and your neighbor as yourself.[54]

Both Francis and Clare understood that, as simple as it seemed, it was the core of the good news, the gospel of our Lord Jesus Christ.[55]

---

[53] BCl 14: *Estote semper amatrices Dei, animarum vestrarum et omnium sororum vestrarum.*

[54] 2LtF 18: *Sed o quam beati et benedicti sunt illi qui Deum diligunt et faciunt sicut dicit ipse Dominus in evangelio: Diliges Dominum Deum tuum ex toto corde tuo et ex tota mente tua et proximum tuum sicut te ipsum.*

[55] Matt 22:37-39; Mark 12:30-31; Luke 10:27.

IV. BIBLIOGRAPHY

Manuscripts and Editions

Bartoli Langeli, Attilio. *Gli Autografi di Frate Francesco e di Frate Leone.* Turnhout: Brepols, 2000. 104-30.

Boccali, Giovanni. *Textus opusculorum S. Francisci et S. Clarae Assisiensis.* Assisi: Chiesa Nuova, 1976.

_____. *Opuscula S. Francisci et scripta S. Clarae Assisiensis.* Assisi: Chiesa Nuova, 1978.

_____. "Testamento e benedizione di S. Chiara. Nuovo codice latino." *Archivum Franciscanum Historicum* 82 (1989): 273-305.

Ciccarelli, Diego. "Contributi alla recensione degli scritti di S. Chiara." *Miscellanea Francescana* 79 (1979): 347-74.

_____. "I manoscritti francescani della Biblioteca Universitaria di Messina." *Miscellanea Francescana* 78 (1978): 495-563.

Claire d'Assise: Écrits. Marie-France Becker, Jean-François Godet, Thaddée Matura, eds. Sources Chrétiennes 325. Paris: Éditions du Cerf, 1985.

Fontes Franciscani. Enrico Menestò and Stefano Brufani, eds. Assisi: Edizioni Porziuncola, 1995.

Omaechevarria, Ignacio. *Escritos de Santa Clara y documentos complementarios.* Madrid: Biblioteca de Autores Cristianos, 1982.

Seraphicae Legislationis Textus Originales. Quaracchi: Collegium S. Bonaventurae, 1897.

BCl = Boccali[76], 193-95; Boccali[78], 404-08; Boccali[89], 293-94; Ciccarelli, 373-74; *Claire d'Assise: Écrits,* 186-89; *Fontes Franciscani,* 2323-24; Omaechevarria[82], 450-53; *Seraphicae Legislationis Textus Originales,* 281-82.

Studies

Bartoli Langeli, Attilio. *Gli Autografi di Frate Francesco e di Frate Leone.* Turnhout: Brepols, 2000.

Borkowski, Mark. "A Second Middle High German Translation of the Benediction of Saint Clare." *Franciscan Studies* 36 (1976): 90-104.

Cremaschi, Giovanna and Agnese Acquadro. *Scritti di Santa Chiara d'Assisi*. Vol. I: Commento. Assisi: Edizioni Porziuncola, 1994.

Fassbinder, Maria. "Untersuchungen über die Quellen zum Leben der hl. Klara von Assisi." *Franziskanische Studien* 23 (1936): 296-306.

Fonti Francescane. Padua: Editrici Francescane, 2004. 1784-1786.

Grau, Englebert. "Die Schriften der heiligen Klara und die Werke ihrer Biographen." In *Movimento religioso femminile e francescanesimo nel secolo XIII*. Assisi: SISF, 1980. 193-238.

_____, ed. *Leben und Schriften der heiligen Klara*. Werl/Westfalen: Dietrich Coelde Verlag, 7th ed., 1997.

de Kok, David. "De origine Ordinis S. Clarae in Flandria." *Archivum Franciscanum Historicum* 7 (1914): 244-45.

_____. "S. Clarae Benedictionis textus neerlandici." *Archivum Franciscanum Historicum* 27 (1934): 387-98.

Kuster, Niklaus. "Das Armutsprivileg Innocenz' III. und Klaras Testament: Echt oder Raffinierte Fälschungen?" *Collectanea Franciscana* 66 (1996): 5-95. [English trans. "Clare's Testament and Innocent III's Privilege of Poverty: Genuine or Clever Forgeries?" *Greyfriars Review* 15:2 (2001): 171-252].

Lehmann, Leonhard. "Der Segen der hl. Klara." *Geist und Leben* 67 (1994): 53-62. [Italian trans. "La Benedizione di S. Chiara." *Forma Sororum* 31 (1994): 303-21].

_____. "La Benedizione di Santa Chiara: Analisi ed attualizzazione." In *Dialoghi con Chiara d'Assisi*. Assisi: Edizioni Porziuncola, 1995. 189-209.

Maleczek, Werner. "Das *Privilegium Paupertatis* Innocenz' III. und das Testament der Klara von Assisi: Überlegungen zur Frage ihrer Echtheit." *Collectanea Franciscana* 65 (1995): 5-82. [English trans. "Questions About the Authenticity of the Privilege of Poverty of Innocent III and of the Testament of Clare of Assisi." *Greyfriars Review* 12 (1998): Supplement, 1-80].

Marini, Alfonso. "*Ancilla Christi, plantula Sancti Francisci*: Gli scritti di Santa Chiara e la Regola." In *Chiara Di Assisi*. Spoleto: CISAM, 1993. 109-56.

Paoli, Emore. "La *Benedictio sororibus praesentibus et futuris*." In *Fontes Franciscani*, Enrico Menestò and Stefano Brufani, eds. Assisi: Edizioni Porziuncola, 1995. 2251-54.

Robinson, Pascal. "The Writings of St. Clare of Assisi." *Archivum Francisca-num Historicum* 3 (1910): 433-47.

Seton, Walter. "Some New Sources for the Life of Blessed Agnes of Bohemia, including some Chronological Notes and a New Text of the Benediction of Saint Clare." *Archivum Franciscanum Historicum* 7 (1914): 185-97.

_____. "The Oldest Text of the Benediction of Saint Clare of Assisi." *Revue d'Histoire Franciscaine* 2 (1925): 88-90.

Ubald d'Alençon. "Le plus ancien texte de la bénédiction, du privilège de la pauvreté et du testament de sainte Claire d'Assise." *Revue d'Histoire Fran-ciscaine* 1 (1924): 469-82.

Vaiani, Cesare. "Chiara nei suoi scritti: La benedizione." *Forma Sororum* 39 (1999): 357-63.

Vorreux, Damien. *Sainte Claire d'Assise: Documents.* Paris: Éditions francis-caines, 1983.

Zoppetti, Ginepro and Marco Bartoli, eds. *Santa Chiara d'Assisi: Scritti e documenti.* Assisi-Padua-Vicenza: Editrici Francescane, 1994.